THE DA
LADY DUCKER

THE DAZZLING LADY DOCKER

Britain's Forgotten
Reality Superstar

Tim Hogarth

Scratching Shed Publishing Ltd

Typeset in Warnock Pro Semi Bold and Palatino

Printed and bound in the United Kingdom by

Short Run Press Ltd

Bittern Road, Sowton Industrial Estate, Exeter. EX2 7LW

Tel: 01392 211909   Fax: 01392 444134

For my wonderful wife Nicola and our daughter Hester.
Thanks for helping to bring Norah back into the public eye.

And our friends in Mykonos who listened to numerous
readings – especially Margo!

Contents

'Who do you think *you* are? Lady Docker?'

•

North country saying, circa 1950

SIR BERNARD AND NORAH DOCKER were the most famous pairing in post-war Britain, second only to young Queen Elizabeth and her dashing consort, Prince Philip. However, unlike the royal couple, the Dockers were brash, vulgar and enormous fun – pioneers of the cult of celebrity.

They lived life at breakneck pace and, as with the reality television stars of today, had publicity showered upon them. Norah used it to her personal advantage, but also to further the companies and products with which Sir Bernard – richest of Norah's three millionaire husbands – was associated.

His extensive business interests included chairmanship of B.S.A. (Birmingham Small Arms) and outright ownership of Daimler, the brand of car with which the Dockers were synonymous. Sir Bernard also held lucrative directorships with leading UK companies, including travel firm Thomas Cook and the Midland Bank.

Amid the grey and dreary austerity of a period still reeling from the Second World War, in a nation desperate for light and frivolity, the 'Dazzling Dockers' were a headline-making machine. The nation couldn't get enough of their antics. Daily newspapers would, in lurid detail, pick through Norah's excessive spending on clothes, furs, diamonds and her notorious gold-plated Daimlers with zebra skin covers. She was banned from Monte Carlo and twice robbed of her jewels, the first such heist becoming the inspiration for Peter Sellers's *Pink Panther* films. Norah and Sir Bernard romped their way through café society, from the French Riviera to London to Palm Beach.

In a blaze of publicity, the Dockers enjoyed a profile most Hollywood stars of their day could only dream about and that attention made even more money. The B.S.A. share price climbed and they could do no wrong. Furthermore, the working man and woman loved Norah. She had the common touch, seemed one of them, happy to talk to anyone. Never grand, she might be caught having a good gossip and a fag with a shop girl, or playing with children in back streets. There were stories of Lady Docker playing marbles in Dior and diamonds. 'Lady Docker down the mines!' shrieked the tabloids after one particular visit to a Yorkshire pit. She then returned the invitation, inviting the miners onto the Dockers' luxury sixty-five metre ocean-going motor yacht, *Shemara*, where they were regally entertained with the finest food, wines and cigars, all served up by Norah herself and filmed by Pathé news. She even gave the delighted Yorkshiremen an impromptu sailor's hornpipe as a bemused Sir Bernard – and viewers up and down the land – looked on adoringly.

Yet none of this could go on forever.

As happened with Marie Antoinette, the last Queen of France, revolution and resentment about Norah's over-lavish lifestyle were brewing. In 1956, Sir Bernard was voted off the B.S.A. board by shareholders; a shock reversal indeed.

The following two decades saw a steep decline in the Dockers' fortunes, during which time they first became a joke then an irrelevance. Times, as they will, moved on. The nation was soon fascinated by a new batch of Swinging Sixties stars like the Beatles, Twiggy and Mary Quant, the papers full of sex scandals such as the Profumo affair. Once vast wealth was lost in the struggle to keep pace with the jetset. Higher taxes and bad investments further drained the pot, meaning the couple's three-thousand acre country estate and superyacht had to be sold on at knock-down prices.

At a conservative estimate, fifteen million pounds had all but vanished by the 1970s, at which point the Dockers had become merely a forgotten footnote in history.

Until now.

1
·
Bright Young Thing

NORAH ROYCE TURNER ARRIVED IN London in the autumn of 1924. Eighteen years of age, she was a little shy and not unnaturally scared. Here was the bustling and prosperous metropolis that would either make or break her.

So intimidated yes, but captivated also. For she knew that if she could make it in England's capital there would be no chance of her ever having to return to Birmingham and the hovel her family called home.

Liberated by the city's vibrancy, Norah simply had to make her mark, the squalor of what she henceforth always condemned as a provincial backwater behind her. She grew enchanted by the windows of Bond Street, Burlington Arcade and Regent Street; hypnotised by those retail emporiums selling the latest fashions, furs and jewellery. Outside Cartier, she was like a child gazing into a toy store, nose pressed against the glass, dreaming of owning the luxuries on display.

But these were daydreams. Many other girls came to London to meet and marry a rich man, so why should she be any different? Norah was just one among thousands of hopeful women looking for the husband who would change her life.

***

LONDON IN THE 'ROARING TWENTIES' was in the throes of the Jazz Age, wherein the rise of gramophones and radio brought American music to the fore, a timely antidote to the anguish and horrors of the Great War just gone. The wounds of 1914-18, however, were still raw, with many young people intent on living for the moment rather than worrying about what the future may bring.

Commerce too was booming. Wartime restrictions were lifted and the city was awash with new and exciting opportunities. Jobs were created and imports and exports hit new highs, while restaurants and clubs opened daily. London shook off its grief for the fallen heroes and was soon trading at the centre of the world again, freshly risen from the ashes.

At the forefront of all this, certainly as far as journalists were concerned, were the 'Bright Young Things', a fabled group of bohemian aristocrats and socialites seldom out of the spotlight due to their drug and drink-fuelled treasure hunts and other such antics. Later to inspire such writers as Nancy Mitford, Anthony Powell and Evelyn Waugh, the sense of danger and excitement they exuded was palpable and, before long, Norah became one of the moths around their candle. She began to frequent the same clubs on the fringes of café society. Dark corners of the city inhabited by these beautiful people who had witnessed first and second hand such bloody carnage and now just wanted a good time.

The Bright Young Things partied as if the end of the

world was only days away, a heady mix of glamour tinged with sadness that Norah found impossibly alluring. 'Live for today,' it said. 'Tomorrow may never come.' Hedonism was in the air and Miss Turner caught the bug.

There was dancing too, and more specifically the craze that swept not just London but the world: the Charleston. Introduced in 1923 by an all-black cast in the legendary *Ziegfeld Follies*, the series of New York City Broadway revues that ran from 1907 to 1931 and for a while moved to radio, it had taken the USA by storm. Churches called it immoral and women's groups frowned upon its frantic up and down movements and racy female 'flappers' in their daring dresses.

Although the marches, hunger strikes and other self-sacrifices of Britain's suffragettes had by 1918 won some women the vote, these were still the early years of female emancipation, an era in which a lack of traditional feminine decorum was deemed shocking. Nevertheless, in London in 1924, clubs were full of women dancing with freedom and abandon, be it to the Charleston, Black Bottom or some other such exuberance. Straight-laced Edwardian society was no more, it seemed. The Charleston, after all, was billed as 'the dance of Negros', its thrusting knees, torsos, hip and pelvic movements openly flouting the prevailing sexual mores.

Still, Norah adored it and the freedom it suggested. She became totally absorbed in the frenetic movements and dreamt of being the next Clara Bow, American 'It Girl' actress of the silent movie era. In fact the silver screen generally was much in her thoughts, as it was for millions of others in the 1920s. Norah admired the starlet Joan Crawford, a former dancer and showgirl, and imagined herself exuding such glamour. She too dreamed of going to Hollywood, making movies and living the dream.

A dream, however, is all it was. The days when the

name 'Norah' was on everyone's lips were decades away and even then not as a movie star. The immediate reality of her move to London was a grim one of hardship and tragedy. Her mother had somehow scraped together £100 – around £5,000 in today's terms – to send her daughter to London and had called in a favour from a family friend to find her a place to live. Mrs. Cumberland had a run-down terrace house in Sinclair Street, Kensington, and agreed to take Norah in as a guest for the sum of thirty shillings a week.

'Auntie' as Norah called the woman, was kind and helpful to her young and naïve lodger. She would give her little pep-up talks from time to time and comfort the girl.

Norah needed a plan, not least because her money wasn't infinite and her clothes were already threadbare. Her single pair of shoes had a hole in them. She could dance, though, and took a fateful decision to enrol for training. This she did at the school of one Colonel Santos Casani, the most famous dance teacher of the 1920s, with premises on Regent Street. His services wouldn't be cheap and nor was he very pleasant. In fact he was a cruel and callous tyrant who reduced pupils to tears on a daily basis. That they endured these ritual humiliations and paid for the pleasure of them was down purely to Casani's reputation as the maestro. He was considered the greatest dancer in Europe no less.

Casani: the man who taught Valentino the Tango.

One of many publicity stunts had been to demonstrate the 'flat Charleston' on the roof of a moving London taxi. The scene was filmed and shown across the country as a vignette to encapsulate the Roaring Twenties and 'Anything Goes' era. It also aimed to demonstrate how the 'flat Charleston,' which required little space, lacked the dangerous vigour of the original, with its risk of black eyes and broken limbs from the frenetic cavalcade of flying heels and arms. Some dance halls were on the verge of banning it. Like silent movie comedian Harold Lloyd hanging from a clock face, Casani dancing on top of a London taxi became an iconic image of the decade.

Casani made many such demonstration films for British Pathé and with fame came the title 'King of Dance,' though some called him 'the Butcher' in his ruthless quest to attract only the best dancers to his school. He demanded perfection and, when it failed to materialise, his temper flared like a firework, reducing all around to quivering wrecks. He ran his studio with a rod of iron, pushing even his most talented pupils to the limits of physical endurance.

And so into this environment entered Norah Turner, with pretty much all that was left of her mother's money in her hand. The girl had average looks, but was blessed with drive and a vivacious personality. Dance offered a chance of achievement and the opportunity to meet the man who could make her rich. She'd seen enough poverty to last a lifetime.

Norah was also aware that without eye-catching beauty she would have to work that bit harder to get to the top of the heap. Her relentless ambition was an asset, as were her slim figure, blonde hair and English rose complexion. But the greatest thing in her favour was her sparkling personality.

Often the most beautiful girls were dull and had no conversation, never needing to work at it. No one could ever say that about Norah. She was a firecracker whose sure sense of herself would create numerous run-ins with her tutor.

The most blazing came one lovely June day, pleasantly warm rather than hot.

Norah was caught looking out of a school window, day-dreaming about the smart shopping ladies and gents in their fine attire lining Regent Street below. Were they going to Liberty? Or heading for stores like Selfridges or Marshall and Snelgrove on Oxford Street, she mused enviously.

'Norah Turner!' Casani screamed. 'Have you been paying attention? Come to the dance floor.'

His face flushed with fury, the great dancer seized her hand and demanded that Miss Turner demonstrate the steps he had just been showing the class. Bemused, his pupil attempted a foxtrot.

'It's not a fucking foxtrot, you idiot,' he shrieked, blood vessels throbbing in his neck. The other girls sniggered at her ordeal and Norah began to cry, which raised Casani's latin temperament to boiling point. 'Stop that now,' he demanded. 'Your mother has paid good money to send you to me. You have the making of a good dancer, a natural, which is more than can be said for some in this studio! Stop daydreaming Norah. Listen and learn or leave.' Furious, his eyes flashed with anger. 'I do not want you to fail. If you fail, I fail and that is not an option. Now dry your eyes and dance.'

Casani had hit the nail on the head. Failure could not be countenanced, by his pupil also.

Her father's last words came rushing back: 'You would be able to care for the family, wouldn't you? They'd all depend on you.'

And so, with a mixture of grudging respect and fear, Norah buckled down to be the best dancer she could be. She danced and pranced until her feet bled. She listened and learned and followed Casani's instructions intently. She was going to be a great dancer, perhaps she would go to America and become a *Ziegfeld Follies* girl? Or be plucked from the chorus to become a movie star? All Norah knew was that she could not let everyone – including herself – down. Casani had spotted a raw talent in Norah and under his tutelage she was soon turning that faith into reality.

Beyond the classroom, Casani's popularity knew few bounds. His demonstration films for Pathé brought him more and more girls and boys who wanted to dance. The numbers grew overwhelming and within months of that outburst he'd offered Norah an opportunity that was to change her life.

'You are my best girl,' he said. 'A natural like Irene Castle. I need you to come and work with me."

It was quite a turnaround and one that at first Norah couldn't quite believe. It hadn't been so long ago that he had reduced her to tears and now here the King of Dance was, pleading for her assistance and comparing her to one of the most famous and influential Broadway and film dancers of the age. Norah was understandably bowled over.

'Yes,' she shrieked, jumping for joy. 'Yes!'

The job – Norah's first – would be commission-based. Casani offered her ten shillings out of every thirty-shilling lesson she gave. With her savings all but gone she desperately needed the cash and the amount sounded like a windfall. However she would soon change her mind about that.

Norah was not a natural teacher. In her memoirs, she speaks of trying to get a shoal of flat-footed rhythmless stooges to dance, while they stamped on her feet. She hated it and became bitter that Casani took the lion's share. The opportunity he had given her began to feel like a poisoned chalice. She hated it and had to move on. Besides, there were no rich and eligible dance partners at Casani's, just spotty youths and hopeless old matrons as she saw it.

Norah's ambitions would always get the better of her. Easily bored, she tended always to want bigger and better and grew tired quickly when it wasn't on offer. She asked Casani for a fifty-fifty split and he refused.

'It's the Casani Dance School, madam, not the Turner Dance School,' he replied. 'They pay for my name not yours.'

'Fine,' shouted headstrong Norma. 'You teach them in that case. I've had it.' And off she went!

The Dazzling Lady Docker

Norah knew there was only one other venue that could make her dreams reality – the famous and fashionable Café de Paris, freshly opened in Piccadilly.

Its exotic promise would be just the thing for an adventurous and lively girl like her – someone with their wits about them – out to bag a millionaire.

One problem though: every other dancer in London had their eye on the Café de Paris too, making chances of employment slim. Norah Turner, though, would land the job she needed and in doing so become the talk of London town.

2
•
Keeping Up Appearances

NORAH WAS 'HIGH-BORN'; THOUGH into surroundings less opulent than those she would come to know. A small flat above a Derby butcher's shop to be precise, on 23 June 1906.

The second of four children born to Amy and Sydney Turner, at heart she found her Derbyshire origins distasteful. But in classic Lady Docker style, she would nevertheless craft the story to its very best advantage. It became her connection to the ordinary man or woman in the street.

Derby back then was a sprawling county town at the height of its Edwardian glory, still surging with the growth in manufacturing made possible by the Industrial Revolution. As with the UK's big cities in that era – a status Derby would not gain until 1977 – its working class folk were thrown together in terraced housing, while wealthier residents and the management class lived in leafy suburbs. Its most famous company, Rolls Royce, opened for business in 1907.

The Dazzling Lady Docker

In later years, Norah would quip that Rolls Royce only began producing their luxury cars in the town because she had just been born there.

The font of such ideas was clearly Amy, her mother, similar to the adult Norah in looks and demeanor and, going by her daughter's own autobiographical account, driven by ambition for a better life at any cost. Amy hated seeing the queues of lowly grey people waiting down below in London Road, eager to get their choppers around 'the best pork pies in town'. So much so that she would walk over a mile to the next butcher's shop so as not to be seen mingling with the 'lower classes'. And yet both she and her husband, Sydney, were of lowly stock themselves.

Little is known about Norah's maternal grandparents. Her paternal grandfather, however, had been a wheelwright, his son and Norah's father rising to become a mechanical engineer. Norah would describe him as 'a self-made man', while stressing her mother's role in urging him in that direction. As Norah tells it, Amy appears to have looked upon Sydney and her brood as a means to one end – her own self-advancement – although raising the family's circumstances would of course have been to the benefit of them all. The extent to which Amy's ambitions were driven by love, fear or individual aspiration – or a combination of all those things perhaps – can now only be guessed at, since the woman herself is no longer around to be asked.

Norah was the couple's middle daughter, two and a half years younger than sister Bernice, and six years older than Alma. Baby of the bunch was Royce, their only son. Of Norah, Amy was once heard to say: 'She's no looker, but mark my words the girl will snare herself a prince one day.'

With such a social climber at the helm, Derby was never going to be good enough for the Turners. Two years after the birth of their second child, Amy insisted that the then family of four leave their little flat and strike out for the big city. Namely, Birmingham, home to the Dockers, a clan regarded among the industrial nouveau riche as near-royalty.

That, though, was for the future. For now, Sidney had his hands full rising to his wife's expectations, a man it would be easy to caricature as hen-pecked. Quite obviously, there was more to him than that however. Sydney had business acumen, if maybe not to the level Amy required. Despite enjoying a steady stream of work as a shop-fitter for Boots the Chemist, who were opening branches up and down the country at the time, his better half had other ideas. He wasn't earning enough, she said, so he set up a new business instead, furnishing the mills and factories of which Birmingham had thousands. Still, the imagined fortunes refused to materialise.

As the arrival of Rolls Royce in Derby suggests, this was also the era in which the automotive industry took hold. Sidney was as fascinated by these new horseless carriages as anyone, realizing that they would revolutionize the world.

One day, he was approached by an agent for the Ford Motor Company, who offered him their dealerships in the midlands. The year the Turners landed in Birmingham, 1908, was also the year when Henry Ford's 'car for the people', the Model T, became the first such mass produced vehicle, his famous mantra: 'You can have any colour you like, as long as its black.' Yet for some reason Sydney declined an offer that would have resulted in him becoming a multi-millionaire beyond even Amy's wildest dreams. By 1927, some fifteen million Model Ts were rolling off Ford's plant in Detroit.

The obvious question is why?

Perhaps Sydney didn't have the start-up funds? Or did he see selling a single brand as too risky? Ford, after all, was not a household name yet. Maybe Amy stuck her oar in, social pretensions preventing her husband from entering the mass market. Norah's rather whimsical version is that Sidney turned those dealerships down because during his one experience of driving a Ford, his foot slipped on the pedal and he hit a brick wall. The true reasons are lost in the exhaust fumes of history, though one thing is for sure. A golden opportunity to finally realise mega-rich big-wheel status was punctured.

Car showrooms, however, stayed in the picture. The idea had now been planted in Sydney's mind, so he opened one of his own, selling a variety of brands to a more upmarket client base. With lots of new money washing around in both the midlands and elsewhere, the venture was a moderate success. Amy was on her way up the social ladder at last.

The first item on an extensive shopping list was a home. The one they bought, the grandly-named Garrick House in a respectable part of the city, was fine, if modest, and the family came to love it. Everyone, that is, except Amy, who soon tired of the place. 'Far too suburban,' she sulked. 'I want bigger and better than this.'

'But Amy,' said Sydney, 'we were living over a butcher's shop last year and now look at us.'

'Well, Sydney Turner,' she retorted. 'This dump may be good enough for you, but it's not good enough for me. I've found us the most divine house. You will love it.'

Sydney asked how they were going to pay for it.

'You will have to sell more cars darling.'

The Turners' duly settled next in Edgbaston, one of Birmingham's most affluent suburbs. With its broad tree-lined streets, avenues peppered with mansions, villas and semi-detached houses, it was built for the upwardly mobile. And any such residence must have a name – Radcliffe House this time, large and elegant. It provided a happy family home until Amy one day saw a young man erecting a 'For Sale' sign on the gate of a still more impressive property.

Edgbaston Park Road was then widely regarded as the smartest location in which to live. Amy gaped through the cast iron posts and saw a vision-turned-reality. 'Rockingham House. Handsomely appointed eight-bedroom mansion, large grounds and servant's quarters,' the sign read.

'Take the sign down young man,' she said. 'I'm buying that house.'

'But madam,' the startled boy replied. 'My boss will kill me if I do that.'

'How will he know?' she said, fumbling in a crocodile skin handbag before pulling out a pencil and silver notepad. She took the agent's details and gave the boy, who was now lost for words, a gold half-sovereign. 'Hide the board behind the wall and be on your way.'

Amy hailed a cab and went to the estate agents and completed the purchase.

***

AMY TURNER HAD ARRIVED. ELEGANT reception rooms, fine drawing room with Victorian fireplace made from the very finest Carrara marble, wood-panelled library, eight bedrooms, two bathrooms, servants quarters and coach house ... Rockingham House was everything she'd hoped.

Elegant calling cards were printed, embossed with 'Mrs Sydney Turner, Rockingham House, Edgbaston Park Road,' dispensed to anyone who would take one. With breathtaking nerve, she would call on Birmingham's affluent elite in the vain hope of being received. Many years later, Amy would admit to having called at the Dockers' mansion and leaving her card. It was a bold exercise doomed to failure.

The Dazzling Lady Docker

Meanwhile, in the wider world, the clouds of war were gathering and Sydney, like many of his contemporaries, rallied to the cause. He decided to enlist in the King's Army, but was rejected by the Medical Board and told he had 'the strength of a postage stamp'. It was a devastating blow to a proud and honorable man who only wished to serve his country, and it caused him great pain and sadness. While all around were on the battlefields of Europe, Sydney sat isolated at home and depression set in. Wrongly believing he had an incurable heart condition and with his nerves in shreds, his business began to falter. No-one was buying cars and as the war rolled on he struggled to make ends meet. Amy, though, seemed oblivious to Sydney's meltdown, both physical and financial. The poor chap was being brought to his knees.

Rockingham House needed a household staff of maids, cook and gardener, the woman of the house decided. The by now four children were dressed in the finest clothes, the girls in fur-lined capes and hats, Royce in sailor-boy outfits. Every day Sydney would be presented with unpaid bills from Birmingham's leading department stores – haberdashers, florists, even the grocer and milkman. Amy's non-stop spending would manifest itself in Norah in years to come.

On the very day Sydney snapped and had a nervous breakdown, Amy bought moleskin coats, trimmed in mink with matching muffs, for her girls, needless frippery.

The two older girls went away for private schooling, to Penrhos College, Colwyn Bay, Wales, though the principality was far from Amy's preference. She dreamed of a governess and Swiss finishing schools for Bernice and Norah, whose poor education was due mainly to her taking very little notice of her teachers. However she did develop a talent that would become useful tool all her life – a keen eye for the opposite sex. 'Boys like me and I like boys,' she was often heard to say. Her despairing headmistress, Miss Harvey, a stern woman of scant sexual allure, called Norah 'wanton' and 'a Jezebel'. Penrhos College was all-girl but there were boyfriends aplenty at nearby Rydal School. Letters flew and the rather racy Miss Turner's humour and natural *joie de vivre* peaked many an interest. Norah craved danger and excitement, very limited in Colwyn Bay other than via the out-of-bounds Tuck Shop. Her scrapes very often resulted in detention, but she continued determinedly doing just what she liked.

Back in Birmingham, however, things were about to take a tragic turn, bringing these school days to an abrupt end. The fragile world in which the Turner family moved was set to crash down like a house of cards. Two years after his first nervous breakdown, Sydney suffered another and the implications were life-changing.

***

IT COULD ALL HAVE BEEN avoided, had Amy cut her cloth accordingly. Her cavalier attitude towards Sydney, money and her right to the very best not only drove Norah's loving father to the edge of the precipice, it tipped him right over.

The clothes, jewellery, house and staff that Sydney could ill afford were part of a reckless pursuit for more and more. That was how Norah saw it anyway. Very much her mother's girl, there was never room for doubt in her mind.

Having broken down again, Sydney was sent away to a private nursing home to convalesce, which Norah reckoned suited her mother though there was at least one other complication afoot. Locally, to add to the pressure of Sydney's money troubles, whispers grew louder about his lack of front-line duty. A caring father and formerly jolly and fun, in

27

contrast to their mother's more intense demeanor, the children wanted desperately their old dad back. That was not however to be and, in his absence, business got even worse. Even as sales of shiny new cars picked up elsewhere post-war, people began to boycott his showroom for the simple reason of his failure to serve king and country. 'There didn't look to be much wrong with him,' Edgbaston chattered.

To make matters worse, Sydney, broken mentally and financially, was then removed from the nursing home as Amy, well aware of the mess now if she hadn't been before, had not paid the bill. So back he came to Rockingham House, or his shell did at least. Out of the door, meanwhile, went the finest items of silver, destined for the pawnbroker's shop.

On his return to Rockingham House, Sydney tottered in clutching a Gladstone bag, packed with his clothing and requisites. He may also have had a bottle of whisky stuffed in there. Many years later, Norah revealed that her dear daddy sometimes sought solace in a snifter or three. Frankly, who could blame him?

It was Easter, 1921, Maundy Thursday in fact, upon which date the reigning Monarch dispenses money to the poor. The Turner family was so far on its uppers that asking King George V for assistance had seriously been entertained, a stigma that would never leave Norah.

She had always been Sydney's favourite child, and as he hugged her in the hallway he spoke in more measured tones than before, but the words were sheer joy to Norah's ears. 'I can't tell you how wonderful it is to be home, darling. Where are all the others?'

Amy, as it happened, was out shopping and having her hair done, flirting with local tradesmen no doubt, to extend her lines of credit – a finely honed art she would teach her middle daughter all too soon. Remarkably, the family still employed a nanny, who had taken Alma for a walk, while eighteen-year old Bernice was out with little Royce.

At the mention of Amy and shopping his eyes rolled in his head. 'Well never mind, Norah. You're here and I will see them all later.'

She was the apple of his eye, his special little girl.

Recalling events later, Norah felt her father looked well enough, contented even, though also a little shabby and older than his 45 years. His hair needed a cut and his jacket was frayed. They strolled arm in arm into the library and Sidney sat in his favourite spot, a battered olive green leather wing chair. He took out his pipe – its amber mouthpiece glistened like gold – and as the smoke began to swirl spoke gently at first, then with more urgency.

'Norah, you are grown up now. If anything happens to me, you would be able to care for the family, wouldn't you? They'd all depend on you.' Norah was flustered, embarrassed, not understanding her father's inference.

'Of course, Daddy,' she laughed, gaily.

Had Sydney detected the ambition in his daughter that would propel her to dizzying heights? We will never know.

However the consequences of that brief conversation would stay with her until the day she died. Norah was just sixteen years old, young and silly with a head full of boys. Daddy was home and she was happy for the moment.

Sydney fumbled for some coins; three half crowns and a sixpence or two. 'Take yourself off to the cinema,' he said.

Ever ready for a good time, Norah took the silver, kissed her father and skipped up the road, where she found Bernice and told her the joyful news. The pair then went to see Lionelle Howard, Manning Haynes and Johnny Butt in a silent comedy adaptation of Jerome K. Jerome's book *Three Men in a Boat*, leaving baby Royce with Alma and the nanny.

29

The Dazzling Lady Docker

The two sisters found the trio's adventures on the Thames hilarious and laughed all way home, arm in arm. Yet when Rockingham House came into view it was a vision of chaos.

There were people everywhere. Police, nursing home staff and a young housemaid in floods of tears. Amy had also returned and was sobbing ferociously herself. Sydney though was gone, along with his Gladstone bag, and everyone feared for what he would do next. Norah reassured anyone who would listen that he was fine: 'Don't worry, he'll be back.'

The doctor blamed Amy for Sydney's disappearance – 'Mrs. Turner, he is not in a position to cope...' – at which Norah's mother retreated to her room, apparently distraught. Who knows her actual emotions ... worry ... shame ... guilt that she had been the cause of her husband's mental breakdown ... the lights of Rockingham House blazed through the night, and the following night too, but still with no sign of Sydney.

Then came a letter arrived addressed to Mrs. Sydney Turner. It read:

> *'My darling wife,*
> *I do not want to be a burden on you and our children. So I*
> *have made up my mind to take my peace between Holyhead*
> *and Dublin.'*

Amy collapsed wailing to the floor. Norah, Bernice, Alma and little Royce huddled together in their grief and tears flowed. Broken by Sydney's disappearance, none of them knew how to handle the situation. They were grieving and bewildered.

More police arrived, along with the press, itching for a juicy story. The family battened down the hatches and tried to stay strong and calm.

Newspapers printed pictures with the appeal: 'Have

you seen this man?' There was no conclusive proof that Sydney was dead, but neither was there any that he was alive. He had purchased a one-way ticket for the ferry to Ireland and his bank accounts were monitored in the hope he would look for funds, but they were never used again.

Amy and Norah made the trip described in the letter, in the vain hope that Sydney had sought refuge with distant relatives in the newly-declared Republic. This was to prove both futile and tragic. The tragedy was compounded by the lack of a clear answer – was he dead or alive? The lack of a funeral worsened their pain. Formerly, though the family was in trouble, Sydney had largely shouldered that burden alone. Now the true position was out in the open and everything was upside down.

Yet out of sorrow comes necessity. Norah knew she must be tough enough for them all, the words of her father still echoing within. The family would depend on her.

3

•

Time Gentlemen Please

SYDNEY'S SUICIDE PILED CALAMITY UPON calamity, Amy's grief compounded by the sudden and shocking reality check. She was now the breadwinner.

Reality and Amy, however, were unlikely bedfellows.

Mingled with her sadness was fury. How could he do this to them? It was question she would keep asking for the rest of her life, seemingly feeling little or no guilt for her part in his downfall. The fact remained that there was no longer any place to hide, the house of cards must be picked up.

Everything the Turners possessed, from the business to Rockingham House itself, to the cars, clothes and household chattels was mortgaged or borrowed on to the limit. Bankruptcy seemed certain, the family one step away from the fearful workhouses that would not be officially abolished in England until 1930. And if the gossip surrounding Sydney's avoidance of wartime hostilities had left the Turners with a social stain, his suicide compounded matters for his wife and children. Their situation could hardly be worse. Norah, who felt it as keenly if not more keenly than any, recalled people pointing and chattering as they walked by. The gist being that their father was a coward for not going to war and his ultimate release an act of cowardice also.

Although Amy had largely failed to make in-roads into Birmingham's gilded echelons, her pretty daughters had at least been keeping the dream of open doors alive. Among the industrial elite, in their mansions and villas on Edgbaston's premier roads, built from fortunes made in the nineteenth century, were more than enough eligible young bachelors for Bernice, Alma and Norah to snare. Now, though, those hopes lay in tatters. No family of note would wish to be connected with the Turner girls and their dreadfully pushy mother. The father had let King and Country down and his family too, as one matron was heard to trill at the bridge table.

For Norah, such humiliation proved character forming. In later years, she would wear her eventual wealth as armour against those who had ill-judged her. Like Amy, her ambition knew no bounds. Both women were relentless in pursuit of their own ends, though Norah was undoubtedly more astute. She vowed after Sydney's death that she would marry into the British aristocracy, conquer London society and laugh in the faces of those backwater Birmingham matrons. But first the surviving Turners needed a survival plan.

To begin with, Amy tried to run the showrooms, a futile exercise since the business had neither cash nor custom and rents were in arrears. Nor had staff been paid, owed months in lapsed wages, so Amy closed it down. Next to go was Amy's beloved Rockingham House. She toyed with the idea of letting rooms, but the income would have been nowhere near sufficient to keep such an exclusive property ticking over. The servants, nanny, cook, house and chamber maids were all given their cards, closely followed by the chauffeur. Rockingham House and its contents went to public auction. According to Norah, Amy shed more tears for the pile that had been her crowning glory than she did for the husband who paying for the place had helped to kill.

The auctioneer's gavel fell time and again on paintings, crystal, household linens ... even the garden tools in the shed were sold. People walked through the home gawping at its lavish decorations and whispering about its effect on Sydney. It took less than an hour to apply the final traumatic nail to this unaffordable luxurious coffin.

Amy realised the high life was over, that she would now have to earn some money, though had no idea how she was going to put a roof over their heads and food on the table. She was however certain of one thing. She would not be going back to Derby to live over a butcher's shop. With everything sold and creditors paid off, a small amount of cash remained to invest in a suitable income stream. That turned out to be a public house – the Three Tuns in Sutton Coldfield – where Amy became the landlady.

For Norah and her siblings, ruination was complete. Alone in her room, Norah would sob for hours. She hated the pub and customers, despised everything they represented. All the finery and frippery was gone, she was now in a single parent family whose mother was doing the best she could.

Better late then never, her middle daughter reasoned. If Amy had offered such practical support to Sydney, perhaps they would not have fallen so low, such anguish averted. One thing was definite, however. Norah refused point blank to pull pints behind the Three Tuns bar.

'Never, never, never,' she shrieked. 'I'm not serving beer to fat old men. It's your pub, you do it.'

In her imagination, Norah planned her escape. She would marry a Duke, live in a palace and wake up from this terrible dream. To make matters even more horrifying, Amy took surprisingly well to her new role, suited to the part. She was chatty with customers, got them to drink more and swell the tills, while flirting outrageously. The locals lapped it up.

From time to time they lapped her up too. Once, Norah caught her mother in bed with one of the regulars. Upset, she could not believe that Amy would betray her darling father that way. Then Amy became involved with another regular and soon it was common knowledge that the landlady at the Three Tuns was free with her favours. Two gentleman callers were married men with young families, leading to a blazing row. Norah branded Amy a homewrecker and harlot. It was shameful. Amy retorted that she had physical needs and sexual desires. Not only that, but it was good for business.

So much so, in fact, that through Amy's sheer grit and determination, and with little or no help from her children, the Turners' fortunes were for a time reversed. Money began to be earned and as quickly spent, with lots of male attention. Amy's grand ideas resurfaced. As far as she was concerned, she was moving back up that ladder. She craved becoming a lady again, having staff and a fine house and wardrobe.

Which is why, in a moment of madness, she sold her cash cow and bought the decaying Swan Hotel in upmarket Tenbury Wells instead. It was a decision she'd rue. Although Norah hated the Three Tuns, inside she knew it was a good business that made money and kept the family in a decent lifestyle. The Swan was a different story. Norah believed the venture was doomed from day one and she was right.

By now, living in a new area, Bernice had indeed been married and the new pub had belonged to her father-in-law, Dick Smith. He could not wait to offload the white elephant on to anyone who would take it off his hands. Confident after the job she'd done with the Three Tuns, Amy felt she could turn the Swan around, then sell up at a handsome profit and move on to the next venture. She poured every penny into renovations that would make it welcoming and hospitable.

Problem was, Amy did not know Tenbury Wells well. Although picturesque, the inn's only clients were the local farmers on market day. Nobody else came in. No tourists, no husbands seeking refuge, just a few blokes in muddy wellies every week for an odd pint. The only pleasant memory Norah kept of the Swan related to Royce's nurse, Miss Moody, who took her little brother on her honeymoon. The venture was a financial disaster.

Once again, when it became obvious that Amy could not continue she was forced to sell the Swan at a knockdown price. The family were again reduced to struggling for income and retreated to a small terrace house in Birmingham that Norah would thereafter refer to as a hovel. With Bernice wed, Alma and Royce were still at school and Amy did any small job she could lay her hands on to make ends meet. She took in laundry, sewing and even the occasional gentleman, much to her and her daughters' shame.

Her mother's dreams of glorious social advancement were further away than ever. What's more, their situation was dragging Norah down too. There was next to no chance of meeting an eligible man in Birmingham now, any reputation the Turners had long since torn to tatters. For Norah, there seemed only one option – to make a completely fresh start. With her mother's good wishes and that £100 in her purse, she one day packed her few belongings and fled to the bright lights. In London, no-one would know either Norah herself or her sad story. No-one would judge or point at her.

It could be the start of a new life.

4

•

The Café de Paris

THE CAFE DE PARIS WAS a playground for the rich and famous long before the term 'jetset' was launched into usage. Destined to become one of the world's most celebrated night-spots, its elegant interiors played host to the great, good and beautiful, from royalty to political heavyweights to show business superstars, a haunt of ravishing decadent opulence.

The famous dancers and cabaret acts made it *the* place to be seen and its success was cemented by an early visit from Edward, Prince of Wales, later Duke of Windsor and, in 1936, destined to abdicate the crown to marry the twice-divorced American socialite Wallis Simpson. Well before then, Edward was often seen at the Café with his squeeze of the time, Swiss-born Lady Thelma Furness. Her twin sister, the equally racy Gloria Morgan Vanderbilt (future mother of fashion designer and artist Gloria Vanderbilt), herself briefly to be engaged to Gottfried, German prince of Hohenlohe-Langenburg, would also tag along. All three would dance the night away under the glittering chandeliers with the cream of European society.

The young Prince and his party never picked up a bill at the Café de Paris, however, their attendance itself priceless. Especially with Edward present and Lady Furness draped on his arm, tables were invariably full. And, of course, the venue was also awash with the Bright Young Things and gorgeous hostesses, the role to which Norah considered herself fated. After all, only the rich would be at the Café de Paris – to attract a man there was to catch a guaranteed million or even billionaire. And then there were the groin breaking cabarets, unrivalled in London. The place even provided the backdrop to one of the greatest silent movies of the era, *Piccadilly* (1929), a rich melodrama simmering with sexual and racial tension. It starred Chinese-American siren Anna May Wong as Sosha, a scullery maid, whose risqué cabaret act eventually makes her a star; a *Cinderella* story that fore-shadowed Norah's own sensational rise to the top.

For all her ambition, the Norah who had first arrived in London, naïve and fearful, could not have got anywhere near the Café de Paris. Even if she had been able to summon up the courage, its owners would most likely have shooed her off as a down and out. However, thanks to her experience under Colonel Santos Casani, a notable society figure himself of course, and the dancing talent she developed at his school, confidence now seeped from every pore. Upon storming out of that place in a huff, it didn't take long for this ambitious go-getter to ingratiate herself at the capital's most fashionable hot-spot. Every evening an array of eligible men of varying age and wealthy background were keen to sparkle and cavort with the crème de la crème of London's dance hostesses, of whom only the most outstanding aspirants could ever hope to reach such an elevated position.

And having risen to it, they fought like cats to stay there, until whisked away by one of those meg-rich suitors.

Stakes, then, were high and on setting the Café de Paris in her sights, Norah's campaign of entry began. To begin with she telephoned the staff hourly, or so she later claimed, regularly enough certainly to ensure that when the telephone rang the staff there knew there was a better than average chance that pushy Norah Turner would be on the other end. Typically, they would reassure her that, yes, her details were on file and, yes, if a vacancy arose she would be considered. Well, that wasn't good enough, was it? Norah knew she was being fed a line and that her details had not been passed onto anyone of importance. A fresh tactic was needed.

She opted to dial the harassment up a level and began to doorstep these same members of staff on the pavement outside, much to their displeasure. To be stopped daily by this little upstart, telling them what a wonderful dancer she was, must have been as irritating as it was infuriating. Yet she was on the right track. The man Norah really needed to see was its maître d', Martin Poulson, formerly head waiter of the Embassy Club, who now had the ear of the syndicate who recruited him – booking agents, choreographers and cabaret producers among them. But given his power to make or break a career, Poulson was inundated with letters, telegrams and unsolicited introductions from girls desperate to hear their high heels click across his parquet floors.

In short, the busy Mr. Poulson had seen every trick in the book and was not to be persuaded, not even by someone as persistent as Norah. Until, for some reason, he suddenly relented and agreed to give her an audition. Maybe her continual attentions pushed his patience to breaking point. Maybe someone else of note with Casani connections quietly intervened on her behalf. Or perhaps there was some other explanation that we can now only guess at, it isn't clear. But when Norah entered the Café de Paris for the first time and stood in front of Poulson, she knew everything depended on what followed. Dressed in a demure little tailored suit and a tiny mink collar to look every inch the lady, she knew she had to make a formidable impression.

Ushered into Poulson's oak-panelled office she was greeted thus: 'Do you ever give up, Miss Turner?'

'No Mr. Poulson. I don't,' she answered, before going on to give him the low down on how, if she had been just a few inches shorter, she could have been the dance partner of Casani, the King of Dance himself. 'He was desperate for it.'

Poulson sat and listened, apparently intently, as Norah chattered on and on about how wonderful a dancer she was, but then stopped her in her tracks.

'You have said enough, Miss Turner. I like you and know you can dance. I've asked questions about you. But are you good enough for the finest nightclub in Europe?' He wasn't sure, he said, so offered her a trial at the Café Anglais, a sister venue to the Café de Paris in Leicester Square.

Although, as we've seen, Norah could not in any way be described as a woman of immaculate beauty, one of the usual entry qualifications, Poulson, it seems, couldn't help but be impressed by her charm and infectious wit. Among the Café's clients, there would be men who might hesitate to ask a more classically attractive girl to dance, but they would not be put off from asking her. She could, in her way, be good for business. Yet shocked that Poulson hadn't put her straight into the Café de Paris, Norah herself was disappointed and, lacking guile, blurted out: 'Can two of my girlfriends from the Casani studio come too?'

Poulson, unexpectedly put off his stroke, stammered his agreement. This girl could get anything she desired.

Norah duly danced for one week at the Café Anglais before being transferred to the holy grail, leaving her pals behind.

Although soon captivated by Norah, Poulson had a strict regime. Young ladies were required to dance with unescorted gentlemen of all ages and nothing more. Their character must remain unblemished. Refined, dignified and blessed with exquisite manners, they were expected to be more like a cross between a debutante and English rose than a 'private dancer'. The reality, of course, was otherwise. In her memoirs, now out of print, Norah talks frankly about how in less respectable establishments they might have been called prostitutes, though still insists on the purity of the girls. There is little doubt, though, that the Café de Paris was a cattle market. Women were dancing for money and receiving expensive gifts for it, so perhaps 'courtesan' best fits the bill.

It would be naïve to think that the foreplay of the dance floor did not lead to the bedroom, despite what Norah would have us believe. Pure is not a description we could use about Norah. From the start, her eyes settled on an array of millionaires, young and old. Among them were scions of some of the finest families in England and Europe ... Princes, Dukes and Earls to industrial tycoons and bankers. Some just wanted to dance and chat, others wanted more. A hostess may not, however, leave the Café de Paris with a gentleman friend under any circumstances. They were allowed to join the man at his table, but only by invitation. To break these rules was to be dispensed with instantly.

Meetings that took place, then, were often clandestine affairs. The man would slip a card to the hostess and whisper a time and place in her ear. Norah speaks openly about this and of how one evening she left the Café de Paris to meet a handsome young gent she had been dancing with all night. He left first and she quickly followed in a London cab to the exclusive Mayfair hotel. As she entered his suite she found masses of flowers and chilled champagne waiting, while the handsome man with movie star looks began to seduce her. The heady scent of flowers and sweet champagne as he smothered her in kisses made Norah light-headed. As he excused himself to go to the bathroom and freshen up, she fled from the swish hotel and out into the street as fast as she could, where the fresh air jolted her awake. Why did she flee this luxury liaison? Or did the event, as outlined, actually take place at all? Perhaps it was merely inserted into her book to reassure its readers in 1969 of her saintly virtue!

However, these were the sort of scrapes that most dance hostesses could find themselves in and it wasn't long before such horror stories got back to Amy in Birmingham, via Norah's landlady, Mrs. Cumberland, by now worried for her lodger. Despite Norah's pleadings to the contrary, the upshot was that Amy soon headed south herself, the better to keep watch on her daughter's behaviour. Norah, after all, was not only the family meal ticket, she was a route back into respectable society that Amy craved.

Mrs. Cumberland had too little room for a mother and daughter, so they lodged in various boarding houses across London's East End. One, overrun by cockroaches, was rather poetically and ironically likened by Norah to the Café de Paris, due to the insects' shiny evening wear.

A small flat in Balham followed. Again it was hardly in the most salubrious area but felt like Buckingham Palace in comparison to the squalor that had gone before. And it was there that, finally, a decent wage began rolling in.

Norah grew ever more popular at the Café de Paris and her bank balance was heading so far upwards that she took the decision to move them into the right part of town. Almost. A charming apartment in a stucco townhouse in Bayswater boasted smart modern furnishings, light woods and fabrics in the latest Art Deco style. Bronze and ivory figures of dancing girls were scattered around in a manner that Norah imagined the well-known American actress, artist's model, dancer and man-eater Peggy Hopkins Joyce would have approved. Norah ate up stories in the newspapers about the men who loved and showered the woman known as 'the Original Gold Digger' with jewels. She was Norah's idol. 'All you need, Norah Turner,' she would say into her dressing table mirror, 'is a millionaire. Reel them in like Peggy!'

The Turners settled nicely into their apartment with its big windows overlooking Norfolk Square. Okay, so it was Bayswater not Belgravia, but every little step was helping mother and daughter back up the ladder, wasn't it?

Norah's favourite comic novel was *Gentlemen Prefer Blondes: The Intimate Diary of a Professional Lady*, by Anita Loos, first published in 1925. In 1953 came a film adaptation starring Marilyn Monroe, and the book clearly influenced the movie *How to Marry a Millionaire*, released the same year starring Monroe, Betty Grable and Lauren Bacall. The story's central character is Lorelei Lee, whom Loos is said to have based on Peggy Hopkins Joyce, equally steely in her pursuit of fortune. Neither Lorelei nor Peggy would take no for an answer. Men were mere play-things and providers of financial security.

Established at the Café de Paris, Norah had an idea. Why not give private dance tuition during the day there? The club did like to have an in-house instructor to help their well-heeled but less rhythmically able clients learn one or two easy steps to the waltz or tango. So Norah put it to the maître d', who was putty in her hands by now. Poulson wavered at first, but Norah talked him round. Had not Edward, the Prince of Wales, learned to dance at the Café de Paris during daylight hours? He had, though alas not by Norah. How might history have been changed then? Never mind Mrs. Simpson, what would the British establishment have made of a lass born over a butcher's shop in Derby?

Norah's earnings were soon substantial. Eighty pounds a week came in from her dance class, while she made £100 a week from dance hostessing in the evenings, the equivalent of £8,000 in modern value. Norah charged a brazenly large amount for her lessons, there being no set price agreed for such services; a girl could ask for as little or as much as she liked. Five dances cost five pounds, and she got it. Poulson told her that no-one had ever dared to charge so much. 'There is only one way to get on, Mr. Poulson,' she replied, 'and that is to make oneself expensive!'

It would be Norah's lifelong mantra. Never undersell yourself. As with Peggy Hopkins Joyce, if a man had money to burn, then let him burn it on her.

One of Norah's wealthiest dance partners was sugar tycoon Sir Ernest Tate, of Tate and Lyle fame. Staggeringly rich, Sir Ernest, who was sixty at the time, thought nothing of slipping Norah a cheque for £200. Sweet. Sir Ernest would buy her mink coats and diamonds, no strings attached, and Norah took all these luxuries with open arms. She doubtless realised, deep down, that a handsome young man from a landed family would never marry Norah Turner from Derby. He'd wed some buck-toothed deb', wouldn't he? But this wasn't a handsome young man and there is no fool like an old fool. The likes of Sir Ernest were more generous, easy pickings. So what if an old gent had roving hands when he might pull out of his jacket a red Cartier jewel box.

Norah further recognised that the one person she must look after at the Café de Paris was Mr. Poulson, who certainly had his eagle eye on her. He once quipped 'sugar is no good for you, Norah,' with a sly wink. She would often buy him well-chosen gifts that kept him in the palm of her hand. A crocodile wallet from Asprey, perhaps, or silk tie from Jermyn Street. Lighters from Alfred Dunhill ... all were small tokens but showed Norah's taste for the smarter end of town.

Norah also knew that the 'little' people were useful information sources. She would grease the palms of doormen and cloakroom girls, barmen and cleaners. Such largesse paid dividends many times over. They forewarned her of wealthy patrons, where the man was staying, what he liked to drink. All of which resulted in her dance partner being bowled over by the attentions of the dazzling Miss Turner. Again, this policy stuck to Norah throughout her life – the people on the ground know everything.

Yet just as all seemed to be going so well, things fell apart. Why that should be invites a good deal of speculation.

In her autobiography, Norah writes that Mr. Poulson had become increasingly tired of the business and fed up with the girls' constant cat fights. So, with great regret, he told Norah and the others that he had 'sold his beloved Café de Paris'. This is said to have occurred in 1932, meaning that Norah's dance lessons stopped at the age of twenty-six, too old, she reasons, to work as a paid dancer. So that was that.

Her days in the glittering Café de Paris were, somewhat vaguely, over.

As a story, however, it won't wash. Not least because Martin Poulson didn't own the place – the consortium who originally employed him did that – it wasn't his to sell. Furthermore, Norah's own departure from the Café de Paris turns out only to have been a short interlude of less than two years. As we will see, Norah winds up returning to the place at the behest of, guess who, Mr. Poulson, who according to her account had earlier sold up and left. She really is the ultimate in unreliable narrators.

The Dazzling Lady Docker

Between the lines then we must go for the real reason the Café did not keep such a popular hostess. Surely Norah, enjoying all the attention and raking in the cash, would never have left through choice. Did someone, Amy perhaps (again unlikely), make the decision for her? Was she just too blatant in her desire to net a millionaire? It is hard to miss the scent of a scandal here, perhaps with a married man? Or even a terminated pregnancy out of wedlock, which could not have been countenanced by a club so dependent upon high class patronage? For Norah adored the Café, the money, the gifts and millionaires. It would have made no sense whatsoever for her to up-sticks without good reason.

More especially so when her chosen bolt hole was the north west of England and a town as staid as London was glamorous – the windswept seaside resort of Southport.

The likeliest answer – for which you, dear reader, will have to wait, and which was destined not to be revealed to anyone before those memoirs were published thirty-odd years later – is as surprising as it was totally out of character.

5

•

The Shop Girl

THOUGH THEIR FLIGHT FROM LONDON was a mystery, there is little doubt about why Norah and her mother were again soon broke. With no Café de Paris earnings with which to fund her lavish lifestyle – and an absence of sugar daddies who might pick up an expensive tab – every penny not yet spent on furs and gowns dwindled alarmingly.

Profligacy – quite possibly egged on by Amy given her past record – had caused a spectacular reversal of fortune.

The appeal of Southport – in its heyday during the late-Victorian early-Edwardian era considered the Bournemouth of the North – is less easy to discern. A cynic might suggest that its reputation as an enclave for newly-retired members of the industrial and mercantile trades, and wealthy ones at that, may have been a factor.

Southport's main thoroughfare is the impressive and broad Lord Street, which runs the length of the town, one mile long. Replete with water features, gardens and the sort of imposing architecture that no less a figure than Prince Louis-Napoléon Bonaparte, the future Napoléon III, Emperor of France, is said to have lived among in 1846, some go so far as to suggest it inspired the tree-lined boulevards of Paris. For sure, Southport has an elegant past, appealing to the nouveau riche for a time. When, in 1932, Norah and Amy arrived, the seafront still boasted its elegant lido and floral hall, but none of that held little if any interest for Norah. She found the town overly sedate and pretentious, as well she might after the bright lights of London's West End.

Still, it was clear she needed a job and the plan now was to make the most of her keen eye for style and fashion and cut her teeth in a shop in the north before ending up in Paris herself, in *haute couture* perhaps. Confidence was always one of Norah's prize assets. In actual fact, she found employment in the family-run Bobby's Department Store, a small chain with more stores in Margate and Eastbourne, though one might surmise that, for whatever reason, those were too close for comfort to London. She earned fifty shillings a week, plus the living accommodation she shared with her mother.

She worked in millinery, on a commission of one penny in every pound spent. In such a sleepy town sales were slow, only two or three hats were sold a day. Norah longed to be back at the Café de Paris earning more than this pittance; on a good day she and Amy, otherwise hungry, were on a diet of baked beans and eggs. And this for someone now used to divine afternoon teas at Claridge's and the Ritz. Her plight though was to get worse. Bobby's required its staff to wear smart attire in store, where they also had to buy it. Norah had purchased a brown satin dress, the most stylish outfit she could find amongst the less than fashionable ranges costing an entire week's wages. Her department head though told her that it must be grey and woollen. Unable to afford a new dress Norah was livid. She raged and resigned on the spot. The store manager, in a vain attempt to calm the situation, asked her to reconsider. He would move her to lampshades, he said, if that would help. Norah's fury hit new heights.

'Lampshades? Hats? What's the bloody difference?'

Just as her irrepressible confidence might open doors, so a wilful disregard for negotiations might have immediate appalling consequences. Norah and Amy were homeless.

The pair decided to return to Birmingham, desperate, unemployed and skint they had no choice. So off they went, lodging with a friend of Amy's in a cramped terrace house that Norah called Dickensian. Once upon a time, they had reached the pinnacle of society here, or so a deluded mother and daughter had believed. Well now, like a bad smell, they were back, only this time at the bottom of the heap.

Contemporaries who were accepting of their largesse in the high days before Sydney's suicide, looked down upon the pair again. In a repeat performance, the Turners were marginalized in a city they had called home. Nowhere would the pain feel more acute and rubbed in than Birmingham.

For reasons that will become clear, Norah still had an image to promote, so needed to find work and find it quickly. She still saw fashion as a way forward and got herself a sales job in a small but exclusive ladies outfitters. Problem was, its clientele had socialized with Norah in happier days. Now they treated her with contempt or, as she experienced it, 'like some common little shop girl'. Humiliated, she applied for a position in Lewis of Birmingham, one of the city's largest department stores. Again, doors opened and Norah, full of it, breezed through. Champs-Élysées here we come!

New staff however faced a hair inspection for nits and lice. Norah was not amused, considering the woman doing it an 'old hag' who wielded a metal comb and took pleasure in messing up her voluminous Marcel Wave. She began to sob. A girl who had danced with princes and dukes had been reduced to a humiliating nit check. She lasted just five hours.

Norah realised now that fashion and retail were not for her, but she still needed a wage. One thing Norah could do was dance, so she brushed up her skills and landed a job as a hostess in the well-known Birmingham ballroom, Tony's.

This was all a far cry from the Café de Paris. The cheap decorations, fake flowers and lurid décor made it look more like a transport caff than an elegant ballroom. The rooms at the Café de Paris smelled of fresh flowers. Those at Tony's smelt of beer and B.O. Customers were worse. No aristocrats, just working class blokes paying to dance with a pretty girl.

At Tony's, men selected their partner from a holding pen, where the girls were kept like livestock in an auction market. Norah was repulsed. Nor were there restrictions on sliding hands. Every customer copped a feel! Norah felt like a cheap piece of meat, then fate struck a chord.

One of her less amorous customers was an engineer named Andrew Fraser. His party trick was to tell fortunes with tea leaves. He begged Norah to let him do hers. Highly sceptical, she nevertheless relented.

'You will return to London, become fabulously rich and titled, and marry three times,' he predicted.

Norah shrieked: 'Tommyrot!'

Probably Andrew was merely telling Norah what he knew she wished to hear. It must have been obvious to all she yearned to return to London. Constantly complaining, she never shut up about hating Tony's and Birmingham ... boring everyone with how exciting London life had been.

Norah, at rock bottom for other reasons too, was about to start wriggling back up that greasy pole.

6
•
Secret Lover

SECRETS WERE HARD-WIRED INTO Norah's persona. One
surrounded the end of her first days at the Café de Paris and
it is safe to say that the rest of her life story was peppered
with subterfuge too. Seldom was a public profile so carefully
and skillfully managed.

Another such secret, most likely related to the first, is
all the more remarkable for the shades of nuance it throws
upon her character – and one that absolutely no-one at the
time knew about, including Amy and Norah's glamorous
friends in London. It was only when she later wrote about
this 'secret lover' that the episode became public knowledge.

The story is astonishing for at least three reasons.

One: the fellow in question lived in Birmingham. Two:
their affair had been on-going while she was first at the Café
de Paris, over seven years in total. And three: the enigmatic
object of Norah's desire was neither rich nor handsome. He

did not shower her with gifts. He was twelve years her senior, portly and verging on fat, with thinning hair. His name was Paul Vacher and he was the love of Norah's life.

Long after the relationship ended, she would write of the chemistry and physical attraction both shared. He was a drug she could not resist, an addiction. When they met, Norah had experienced many romances, schoolgirl crushes to begin with, and also a semi-serious relationship with a chap called Bertie Wren. It was Bertie who took young Norah to her first Royal Ascot. Nice idea, you might think. He obviously knew her mind. No. His mistake was failing to gain admittance to the Royal Enclosure, as she complained to Patrick Power, heir to a Birmingham industrial fortune, later.

And so it was Patrick who got to pop the question, with a three-stone diamond ring. It may have weighed that much too. Delighted, Norah accepted, only to discover that her new fiancé had a string of girls at his beck and call, so she called the engagement off after three months. With the handsome and rich Mr. Power dumped, and only just over a year into her London adventure, on a visit home she encountered Monsieur Paul Vacher at a dinner dance at the Queen's Hotel where, in 1925, he had been appointed hotel manager.

His first words to Norah were reportedly: 'So, this is the table where the beautiful blonde lives, *n'est-ce pas?*'

Clearly, being French, he had *la langue pendue* – the gift of the gab – himself. Electricity fizzed as though someone had flicked a switch. It was love at first sight. Norah, at that time, was still forging her personality ... manipulator of men ... courtesan ... all of that was in the brewing, there was still a kind of innocence about her. However that same evening, Paul took her virginity in his room, about which Norah wrote frankly: 'The Frenchmen, let's be honest, are the only ones who really know how to make love to a woman.'

Infatuated, Norah was 20 and Paul was 32. Since his arrival on British shores he'd become experienced in the hotel industry and bedded many women. What he lacked in the looks department he made up for with accomplishment in the bedroom. He knew which buttons to press and when to press them. He was caring and considerate and many of his lady friends, like Norah, came back for more. Yet when Paul proposed marriage, it was to this wannabe dancer from Derby who, ambitious or not, immediately agreed. Paul did though ask Norah if their union could wait until she became 21. Again, Norah acceded to the wish. She was smitten and would do anything to please him. His Gallic charm could turn her into a quivering wreck.

In 1969, Norah wrote openly about it. She was fulfilled, she said, and felt no guilt at having sex outside marriage, even in the mid-1920s. They would be together forever, she was sure, but anyhow, this was about taking female emancipation and running with it. Well, to a point. For as their interactions continued on visits 'home' over the next all-but decade, her career at the Café de Paris was developing fast. Was it by chance that the end of her first spell there was in 1932, just over a year before the eventual end of this affair? But if so, why choose first to go to Southport, not Birmingham? Although, as the reader will recall, mother and daughter did soon end up in Birmingham, didn't they? Perhaps Amy was simply fed up of heart-sick Norah's bleating – maybe that was the root of her unhappiness in the town and subsequent disillusionment with a life in *haute couture*? Indeed, maybe that's why she'd fancied Paris in the first place. As ever with Norah, we are left with more questions than answers.

The bottom line is that she kept her romance with Paul completely to herself. For the most part, it remained a long-distance romance and Norah did the running. Vacher would say: 'Come to Birmingham, darling,' and she would drop everything, unable to resist.

The energy of her lover gave Norah all the love and acceptance she needed but there was one person who could not and would not accept the relationship – Paul's mother. As ever in Norah's story, another woman was to blame. Madame Vacher controlled every aspect of her son's life. He was a mummy's boy and when she said '*saut*', Paul would ask '*quelle hauteur*?'... how high. Though witty and charming, in Norah's eyes he was completely in the control of his mother, who hated her prospective daughter-in-law and everything she stood for. The feeling was reciprocated.

Norah's anguish at this situation may well have been the thing that hardened her sense of purpose. Despite, this disapproval, Norah truly believed that Paul would ditch his mother rather than her and that the pair would one day live happily ever after. Like every fairy tale, there was a wicked witch who simply had to be overcome, that's all. Paul would be the only person Norah ever considered marrying for love. Thereafter, disillusioned perhaps, only cash would count.

Madam Vacher saw Norah as unsophisticated, lacking refinement and any sense of style. Worse, she was common. Common! Nobody ever called Norah that. Time spent in each other's company must have been an absolute ordeal. In a vain attempt to please the woman, and her fiancé, Norah took up piano and singing lessons. He was a talented operatic singer and thought the idea wonderful. He dreamed of himself and Norah performing duets for his operatic group. Alas, Norah had no aptitude for it and so that, mercifully, was that.

Another issue was that Norah still had no money and little chance of earning any, as it seemed at the time. Madame Vacher was only happy when Norah returned to Casani in London, shouting '*Saloup*' (whore) at her as she left the house.

One piece of drama involving Madame Vacher made her both laugh and despair. As she walked into the room one day the elderly woman simply collapsed. Paul howled: 'What have you done to make her faint?'

A doctor was called, but a chuckling Norah just took a drag on her cigarette and replied: 'It's nothing that a bucket of water over the old bitch wouldn't cure!'

Sparks turned into a raging inferno, with Vacher piggy in the middle. Sometimes literally, as when Norah threw a cake at his mother in retaliation for some cruel remark. Norah called the engagement off, and did so many times, before fleeing back to London to lick her wounds. On her next visit, they would kiss and make up while Madame Vacher fumed and plotted how to break them up again.

She won in the end. Norah grew tired of the fights and the non-break-ups and make-ups. Madame Vacher throttled their love, she was certain. After one such fall-out, the matriarch had a letter breaking off the engagement drawn up and told Paul to sign it. Her son, never one to argue with his mother, obliged, handing the paper to Norah while the old woman looked on. She knew that his fiancée's signature would prevent any claim for breach of promise and while the normally headstrong Norah would have torn the letter into shreds, this time she just laughed in Madame Vacher's face as she signed on the bottom line, defiant on the outside – what an exciting future she would make, a life that Paul would now miss out on – but broken inside.

One more secret she must keep to herself...

Crushed, Norah walked the streets of Birmingham, tears streaming down her face. Her world crashing down. Oblivious to the noise and hubbub of the city, she somehow found a pokey little room at fifteen shillings a night. And a night would be all she required. Just like her adored father, she decided to take her own life. With no great prospects yet in London, she felt unable to carry on.

On a grubby bed, she opened her purse and took out a bottle of asprin. In the tablets went, one at a time, like sweets, while she chased them down with a glass of water, ready for death. In her book, she claims to have swallowed over twenty of the things before throwing the bottle against the wall of a dump in which she was determined to end her days. Closing her eyes, she lay down in a foetal position and, having not bothered to write a suicide note, fell to sleep.

Who would have cared enough to read it, anyway?

Next morning, light streamed in through the skylight and onto her waking face. She stared about the room with its single bed, washstand and mirror. Norah was alive and fit as one of its fleas, which she took as a sign that her time was not yet meant to be up. So off she skipped back to Paul's house, where the pair apologised and rekindled their engagement!

In the end, Paul did finally name the Big Day. However that was only upon the untimely death of Madame Vacher (we must assume that Norah had nothing to do with it, even though she would have been scrambling about back in Brum by then!) and for his fiancée that was just too little too late.

She was no longer blind to his weakness, Paul's mother still dominating her shattered son from beyond the grave. If he'd had to wait until Madame Vacher's demise to commit to their union, then what did that say about his real intentions or masculinity? Now, she looked upon him with pity, not adoration. It had taken almost a decade for her to realise that she would not, after all, wed this lowly hotel manager.

Stuff Lewis of Birmingham, stuff Tony's Ballroom and stuff Paul Vacher. London was calling her once more.

In any future relationship, hers would always be the upper hand.

7

•

At Home with Judges and Dukes

WHATEVER THE COST, NORAH COULD spend not one minute longer in the midlands. Taking a cue from *Gentlemen Prefer Blondes*, her favourite book, she told Amy they were off. Within weeks, she was dancing in the capital again.

This time she found work as a dance hostess at the Savoy on the Strand. Was her luck changing again? Opened in 1889 by Richard D'Oyly Carte from huge profits generated from staging Gilbert and Sullivan operettas at his nearby theatre, the Savoy was Britain's first luxury hotel. There were electric lights and lifts, lavishly appointed bedrooms with hot and cold running water in the bathrooms. The manager was one César Ritz, who would eventually own a famous hotel himself. The chef was Auguste Escoffier, famed restaurateur and later culinary writer, a stellar trio to be sure. One might imagine that Norah would adore the place. She loathed it.

Among her many issues were low wages of only five

pounds a week. At the Café de Paris she earned the same sum for teaching five dances. The Savoy had strict house rules too, which infuriated her. Girls could not charge a fee for a dance with an escort, nor could they accept drinks or sit with the gentlemen. There were no fringe benefits, just the pay packet.

Norah felt trapped in a gilded cage and when it was suggested that she should go from her artificial blonde back to her natural brunette she fumed: 'I'm staying just as I am and as I've always been. If you don't like it, you can lump it!'

Like Lorelei, Norah knew the preference of gentlemen.

She moaned bitterly about her plight to anyone who would listen, most often her mother, Amy, who had travelled south with her. She would remind her daughter of the hell at Tony's and Birmingham retail but still Norah complained about the lack of cash, meanness of management, leftover food and so on, detesting the place. Maybe she was lovesick.

Many years later when she was Lady Docker and once again the toast of London's café society, she would give the Savoy a wide berth, preferring the elegance of Claridge's for its convenience to Bond Street and her favourite stores.

Fortunately, Norah's contract there was for two months only and just as it was coming to an end she bumped into an old friend from her Café de Paris days. Lord Graves was a charming rake, an Irish peer with a keen eye for the ladies.

'Well, well, well, if it isn't Norah Turner,' he said. 'How the devil are you?'

'Lord Graves,' she said, 'how lovely to see you again. It's been ages. Do you still go to the Café?'

'I do indeed,' he replied, 'but you don't look happy. Can I treat you to a drink and supper at the 400 Club?'

That was just the tonic Norah needed.

And so Norah and Lord Graves hailed a black cab and headed to a basement in Leicester Square, another place haunted by the rich and famous. Named in reference to the four hundred genuine New York socialites who supposedly could fit into Caroline Astor's ballroom, in later years the 400 Club could number Princess Margaret among its regulars (Mrs. Astor's nephew, Waldorf, was the husband of Nancy Astor, the first female Member of Parliament to take her seat). The regular table for the Princess and her crowd, meanwhile, was dubbed the Royal Box.

On walking into the 400 Club, the first person Norah saw was Martin Poulson, as delighted to see her as she was him. She filled him in on her plight at the Savoy and how much she hated it. Being a man of few words, his reply was music to her ears. 'Would you like to come back to the Café de Paris, Norah?' She flung her arms around him in joy.

'I would love to, Mr. Poulson. When can I start?'

'Tomorrow,' he said, 'and don't be late!'

Again, this is Norah's version as committed to print. The reality may well have been otherwise. A suspicious mind might consider her return to London a little too neat, a mere two-month contract at the Savoy on arrival equally so. Was it all about some unnamed earlier scandal now blowing over? The coincidence of these meetings may have been anything but – if indeed they took place at all. However, let us take her at her word and report that when Poulson's sophisticated figure moved up the stairs and out into Leicester Square, Norah knew she was returning to the place she loved most: the Café de Paris. In the 400 Club, she danced with Lord Graves, tossed back a few drinks and then dashed back to the Savoy to tell them she was leaving, whereupon the hotel's Head of Entertainment informed her she must work a week's notice or forfeit her week's wages. This was the final insult.

'Stick it,' she retorted. 'Buy yourself a packet of fags.'

The Dazzling Lady Docker

***

FROM THE DAY NORAH RETURNED to the Café de Paris, the money and perks she so adored started rolling in again. A cheque for hundreds of pounds here, a mink jacket or a diamond clip there ... the clients gave and Norah took.

Mr. Poulson too was pleased to see her back and gave her the responsibility of organising the cabaret acts. This she was not so keen on, realising immediately why it had been delegated. Artists were tricky to deal with, temperamental, and the Café de Paris prided itself on star turns. One such was a fabled jazz singer and movie star who Norah had to coax her to the stage with a large gin and tonic and sometimes even this didn't do the trick. Otherwise, being back was almost total bliss.

Once again, she danced night after night under those glittering chandeliers, wearing the finest gowns money could buy, at the epicenter of high society. Her coffers were swelling with the spoils and again began to treat all this money with lavish contempt. Dance partners were treated the same way. One of these was a High Court judge, Cecil Whiteley. The judge and the showgirl were an unlikely pairing, but Cecil grew besotted by flirtatious Norah. She wrapped him around her little finger and he adored her for it.

Cecil Whiteley was the 'Common Serjeant' for the Old Bailey and an enviable career at the bar had also seen him rise to become a KC (King's Counsel). In 1915, he had appeared for the prosecution in the notorious trial of George Joseph Smith – aka the Brides in the Bath murderer. Smith was a bigamist and serial killer who had dispatched three women and paid the ultimate price himself. A guilty verdict sealed Whiteley's reputation as a feared and respected courtroom opponent. Smith appealed but that was dismissed and he was sentenced to death, hanged in the yard of Maidstone prison. It made Cecil Whiteley the most famous lawyer – and by the 1930s High Court judge – in the land. A kindly man, he was nevertheless uncomfortable thereafter about donning the black cap, as the law required with capital punishment. Cecil's opposition to it was total. He longed for its abolition but, sadly, died before he could see that come to pass in 1965. Nights at the Café de Paris helped him to relax and unwind.

Once Norah got him in her clutches, he began to act like a lovesick teenager. Cecil would go every evening just to get a glimpse of this brash hostess. He was, however, married to a wife who in the classic complaint 'didn't understand him'. In Norah he found solace, both at the Café and her smart new flat in Queen's Court. There they would drink whisky while Norah listened patiently to his woes about the strain he was under in his judicial work. Norah believed Cecil was on the edge of a nervous breakdown; she read the signs from her father, Sydney. She cared for him, looked after his wellbeing and helped him to forget his responsibilities for a while.

Cecil was desperate to make Norah his mistress. He lavished gifts upon her daily, giving her the most unusual and expensive gift she had thus far received – a hotel for her to run herself. Yet in her later recollections she denied they were lovers, just very good friends. What is one to make of that? Like everything else in Norah's tale, it must surely be taken with a quarry-load of salt. And in and among all these stories too, there must be doubt about the timings. Any one of these men – these sugar daddies – might be the reason for her original departure from the Café de Paris, mightn't they? With only her word to take for it, we simply cannot know.

A real feather in Norah's cap was that rare breed in English aristocracy, a Duke. And not just any old Duke either. Charles Spencer-Churchill, ninth Duke of Marlborough, scion of the famous dynasty and custodian of one of England's finest country houses, the monumental Blenheim Palace in Oxfordshire. Awarded in 1705 to John Churchill, the first Duke of Marlborough, by Queen Anne for his victories in the War of the Spanish Succession, it was named for the final victory at Blenheim. Designed by Vanbrugh and set in an estate of thousands of acres, it more latterly became famous as the birthplace of Sir Winston Churchill in 1874. Not long after that, the family found themselves in dire financial straits and their home's magnificent art collection, silver, jewellery and land was sold. Even then the day was only saved when, in 1895, the ninth Duke of Marlborough married railroad heiress Consuelo Vanderbilt, Gloria's aunt, the sort of socially advantageous but loveless marriage that was common in those days. Consuelo's mother, Alva, was desperate to have an English duke in the family, even if he was penniless. The bride – said to have sobbed behind her veil – did produce two children: the all-important male heir, plus a spare. Divorce followed and the Duke remarried, but the second union was not as lucrative and again the marriage came to no good.

When Norah met the Duke – nicknamed, with delicious irony, 'Sunny' – he was in his sixties and on the hunt for a mistress, no more Duchesses! A deeply gloomy man, he was known for his lack of generosity, a trait Norah abhorred in anyone. He was difficult, cantankerous, set in his ways and immensely stubborn, with a legendary lack of manners. After a dance he would give Norah a £1 tip which she would then, insulted, hand over to one of the waiters as a tip on her part, in full view of the Duke.

One weekend, Sunny did however invite Norah to Blenheim Palace, an offer that thrilled Norah. Dinner in large halls off the family silver ... servants hovering ... it would be a fairytale weekend. She was in for a rude awakening.

On her arrival, Sunny offered to cook for the pair.

'Haven't you got a chef?' Norah asked in amazement.

'Alas no,' replied the Duke. 'One only occupies a small flat in the palace, within which there are no staff.'

Norah couldn't believe her ears. What was this? Bedsitland? However, Christmas was on its way and she kept her dates with the Duke despite coming to detest him. A lavish gift had been promised and she dreamed of priceless jewels, left by the Vanderbilts maybe, awaiting crumbs off the table.

Of course their ultimate coupling was always unlikely, Norah merely a bit on the side, and anyway she claimed to care deeply for Cecil Whiteley. The jealous and gullible judge told her to put the Duke out of the running and marry him instead. But when December 25 arrived, Sunny came up trumps, giving her an onyx-and-diamond-studded cocktail watch. What divine generosity from the old miser! Formerly on the wrist of a Vanderbilt, she surmised, but later looked at it a little closer and saw that it was broken.

'The tight old sod!' she howled, livid.

Norah ran to Cecil's flat in floods of tears. 'How could he do this to me?' she wept. The judge reiterated that the Duke was a skinflint who did not deserve to be seen around town with a beauty like her. He went to his desk, opened it, and produced the jewellery box that he presented to Norah.

'Happy Christmas, darling,' he said.

As she opened it, the light caught on another cocktail watch, ablaze with diamonds. The Duke's looked like it had come from Woolworths by comparison. Norah gasped with joy and planted a huge kiss on Cecil's leathery cheek.

But now she faced a problem when dancing at the Café de Paris – making sure she wore the right watch for the right beau. Thankfully, the Duke then became a Roman Catholic and, in a fit of pique over some small disagreement or other, disappeared from the Café de Paris scene and, as a direct result, from Norah's life.

Cecil Whiteley was delighted he had seen off the Duke of Marlborough. He could now woo Norah to his heart's content. Norah too was relieved the Duke was gone. She had grown to detest the fellow. But Cecil was getting keener and keener and one evening, on their way to dinner, a man born in 1875 and so fast approaching sixty years old got a little too amorous in the cab. Norah was unimpressed, compelled to tell Cecil that she never wanted to see him again. Was she just teasing him? Or were they indeed having an affair?

In any case, the split was short as Norah knew how to be aloof just long enough to get the desired effect. Cecil would call on the telephone begging forgiveness, but Norah would hang up. The next day an expensive gift would arrive at the Queen's Court flat. Another call would follow with an invitation to dinner at a smart bistro, followed by dancing at the 400 Club. There he would promise no repetition of his previous conduct. Norah would relent. She often felt that Cecil's words had real meaning, not just empty promises. To keep Norah, Cecil often said: 'Can't we just stay friends? I don't want to lose you,' and Norah would agree. Not only was Cecil very generous, it seems she genuinely liked him. He was a kind and a good man, so their friendship deepened and remained strong until his death, aged 67, in 1942.

In her book, Norah says she would have liked to say they were lovers but could not, as she didn't love Cecil in the way that he loved her; a fact she felt acute guilt over. It's hard to imagine, though, that her sexual prowess was not a factor in his obsession. The Judge was in complete awe of her. Norah's allure after all landed her with Cecil's very generous gift – the hotel – though his desire to wrest her from the paws of other admirers at the Café de Paris is a believable motive.

The Royal Mount Ephraim Hotel in Royal Tunbridge Wells was built as a country house in 1766. It had thirty-five bedrooms, elegant reception rooms and a bar, all handsomely proportioned. In its heyday, Edward VII adored the town and gave it the Royal prefix in 1909, making it one of only two towns thus honored, the other was Royal Leamington Spa.

Memories of the Swan at Tenbury Wells had clearly not put Norah and Amy off the idea of owning and running such an establishment, for the two of them jumped eagerly at this new opportunity. Anyway, the difference now was that the Turner's had a wealthy benefactor with deep pockets, happy to pick up the tab for what rapidly became another orgy of excess. One trademark Norah quip was: 'If someone else is paying, I will have everything,' and she did! Norah's hotel must appeal to the most affluent clientele and she set about its modernization in earnest. She successfully applied for a licence to sell alcohol, by flirting outrageously in silver fox furs and a black veiled hat with the local JP. Tunbridge Wells, prim and proper, had seen nothing like racy Norah Turner.

Her plan was to run the place in the style of one of the smart Mayfair hotels. She engaged a barman from Grosvenor House, one of London's finest such establishments and set about designing the Royal Mount Ephraim to her notions of sophistication. Out went the functional Edwardian furniture and in came faux French gilded and marbled tables, mirrors, chandeliers, flock wallpaper and such. An elegant Edwardian hotel was replaced by a replica of Madame de Pompadour's boudoir during the reign of terror. Such a flight of fancy horrified rather than impressed the genteel residents.

Unflattering tales spread around town about the overly made up tart being kept by a rich London judge. Many locals complained that you had to put on your best togs to go in. Norah denied that but did throw customers out who lingered too long over a drink. One called her a tart to her face and she bounced him off the premises herself, dumping him on the pavement. Women in the local shop were heard to say: 'How come every time she goes to London she comes back with a new carpet?' The inference being that she would do anything for a roll of Axminster.

All these lurid tales cut Norah deep. The truth no doubt hurt as lonely old men do not buy young women hotels for nothing. Gold letters over the entrance spelled 'Miss Norah Turner', and above her name was the town's coat of arms, burnished to catch the sun in gold. Norah thought it divine and vowed that one day she would have her own coat of arms, and have it emblazoned on everything.

But Norah's lack of business acumen meant the hotel was soon losing money at an astonishing rate. Accounts were in disarray, every day creditors called to demand payment. All of this echoed Amy's exploits, first with Sydney and then her own hotel. Unlike Amy, Norah had a safety net. She was often heard to say: 'Charge it to Judge Whiteley, at his Chambers in Lincoln's Inn Fields. If you can't find him there, try the Old Bailey.'

One ill-fated idea Norah had to boost revenue was to organise a dinner dance, just as in all the top London hotels. She went to great expense and hired her old coach Santos Casani as the star turn. Santos agreed to bring his own band so the guests could dance the night away. Only problem was it looked like there was going to be no guests. Norah failed to sell a single ticket. No-one in the town wished to patronise a hotel run by a fast bottle-blonde hussy from the Big Smoke.

Norah called a former dance partner from her Café de Paris days who lived locally at Ticehurst. His name was Percy Johnson, son of Samuel Meggitt Johnson, who co-owned Bassett's sweet manufacturers, famous for liquorice allsorts.

Percy bought every ticket at 8/6 to help Norah and ensured that the place was filled with house guests from his mansion. Everyone had a ball and it was a major success. Phew!

But the reality was that this could only happen once. Percy could not bail her out of another empty dance floor. How long could she go on? She had twenty-six staff on the payroll, a big commitment in itself. And increasingly Norah was irritated by them and their lazy ways, their humdrum lifestyles and daily petty rows. Norah was already losing interest when the head waiter absconded with the takings, leaving no money with which to pay anyone. By then it was all too apparent that the hotel's owner was unsuited to the cut and thrust of business life. With the help of free-spending Amy, it took her just eighteen months to bankrupt the place.

The bailiffs moved in and the Turners moved back to London, bankruptcy proceedings pending. Hotel chattels were sold at public auction and the proceeds cleared most of the debts. Norah must have looked at this new situation as déjà vu, so closely did it mirror Amy's past plight. She had to go see the Official Receiver at Somerset House, who she clearly charmed because the affair was sorted quickly after that, though a cheque from Cecil for the outstanding amount may also have helped!

In fact, Cecil would come to the rescue again and again, like a knight in shining armour. At one point he discovered that Norah had acquired reams of tickets for parking offences across London over a lengthy period of time. Norah believed she could park wherever she wanted, hurtling around town at full pelt in her little Daimler. However the litany of offences landed Norah in the dock of Marlborough Street Magistrates Court, before the Justice of the Peace, Mr. Sandy Sandbach. He threatened her with jail for contempt of court when she answered back and mocked the Bench. When rebuked for impertinence she just shrugged her shoulders. Then an usher came forward with a note from Judge Cecil Whiteley, the case was dismissed and Norah walked free. Pinned to her car outside, meanwhile, was a parking ticket that Norah then tore into tiny pieces, laughing as she threw them in the air.

Norah Turner was above the law.

That evening, over drinks, she told Cecil she'd had no fear of jail if the Old Beats had sent her down. She needed a diet! Cecil quietly rolled his eyes. Norah believed he could get her out of any scrape, but all this help came at a price. Every evening Cecil would plead with her to marry him.

'Can't we just be engaged, darling, for one night?'

'No, Cecil. You are married, you silly boy!'

Despite this, the judge bought Norah a stunning evening gown and ermine cape and then announced their engagement to a packed Café de Paris.

Cecil's home life was unhappy. Opening his wife's post, he learned that she had a secret lover, a soldier based in Aldershot. With her eye off the ball, Mrs. Whiteley had failed to pay any trades people in the town for over a year and for their part they had not dared to approach the eminent High Court judge. Mrs. Whitley had, however, been sending money to her young man, echoing her husband's behaviour.

Cecil was a great believer that upon release prisoners should be rehabilitated, helped into jobs and homes in order to get their lives back on track. Every year he organised a fête in the large grounds of their Surrey mansion with all proceeds going to charities in that regard. The fête raised over £4,000 and Mrs. Whiteley was in charge of the distribution of funds. This particular year, Cecil received a call from one such charity pointing out that no money had arrived. Confronted, his wife broke down in tears, confessing she had squandered every penny. Cecil, blind to his own faults, could not believe she had committed such a wicked act of betrayal. He asked his wife for the divorce that would let him to marry Norah. But she refused point blank. The embezzlement broke Cecil, who broke down in tears on the shoulder of his lady 'friend'.

Cecil ensured all the charities were paid the proceeds of the fête, his sense of honour allowed nothing less. He told Mrs. Whiteley if she'd come in front of him in his courtroom he would have been duty bound to sentence her to six months in jail.

8

•

Thanks A Million

PAUL VACHER HAD BEEN CONSIGNED to the dustbin of history. Emotionally battered, Norah vowed never to lower her guard again and had been as good as her word.

Time does have a habit of marching on, however. And by 1938, when Norah was 32 years of age, so no longer at her youngest, many more pretty girls were moving up the ranks, all chasing the very thing she was – an elusive millionaire. Yet War again loomed and dance partners were increasingly thin on the ground. Money became tight and with the clock ticking both for the world and Norah herself, it was clear the Café de Paris could not carry on as before. She would have to move fast to snare a man capable of keeping her in the style to which she was determined to become accustomed.

As ever, Norah's trump card was her personality. Witty, bright and intelligent as ever, even as Adolf was ranting on the radio she radiated *joie de vivre*. Many of her counterparts at the Café de Paris may have been younger and prettier, but Norah would always win out over those who could barely string a sentence together. She was chatty and engaging, and a graceful and elegant mover in the style of Ginger Rogers.

The extent of her charm came to the fore when she met the first man she'd marry, Clement Callingham, chairman of Henekeys, noted wine merchants and vintners. The company had been founded by his ancestors over two hundred and seventy years ago – such provenance! Filthy rich and with a plush mansion in Belgravia's Chester Square, Clement had almost everything that Norah was looking for. Sadly, the house in question was occupied by Pamela, the estranged Mrs. Callingham, and the pair's fourteen-year old son, Guy.

Clement cut a sad figure in the Café de Paris. He was looking for love, but the complications were legion. Along with having a wife and child in town, Norah found him dull. For his part, he loathed freckles and she was covered in them. With make-up and long evening gowns, gloves and capes she could conceal them to some extent but took it as a personal affront, anyway. Yet when they danced all of that slipped away. Two became one as they glided across the dancefloor.

For all his faults, Clement's dancing was magical and he cut such an elegant figure. Dashing and immaculately clad in the best of Savile Row and Jermyn Street, his handsome features were complemented by silver-grey hair and eyes of deepest blue. He was tanned and slim yet radiated sadness night after night, sat by himself, downcast and forlorn.

Pamela, meanwhile, inhabited a social whirl. She held cocktail parties and entertained lavishly, the cream of London society clamoured to attend her soirées. Among her guests was the Pennsylvania playboy and amateur golfer Charles Sweeny, husband of the future Margaret Campbell, Duchess of Argyll, who in years to come would scandalise high society with her salacious divorce from her second husband, the eleventh Duke of Argyll, who produced Polaroids of his wife engaging in sexual activity with 'a headless man'.

Pamela adored such hedonism, fuelled by alcohol and drugs. Clement despised it! Serious minded, he liked to read Shakespeare and attend Church. The marriage had dissolved before their eyes, with Clement aggressive and depressed and moving out into Chester Square mews, behind the mansion.

It was there the bookish gentleman and racy hostess became an item, living in sin. In today's world, no one would bat an eyelid at that – or for that matter sexy photos that, if anything, might see you featured in a celebrity magazine. In 1938, such behaviour was scandalous. Doors would close to out-of-wedlock couples; they would be excluded from the social scene. What's more, the women were always to blame, for being fast and loose.

Norah hated all the chattering but had to tough it out if she was going to be the second Mrs. Callingham. As in any relationship, there were aspects of Clement Norah did not find easy. A bookworm she wasn't, and meanness was a trait she abhorred in anyone, especially a supposed lover. Despite this, she hung in there but trouble, again, was brewing.

It came in the shape of the telephone calls, letters and cables she began to be bombarded with daily from Paul Vacher, pleading everlasting love, begging forgiveness and again proposing marriage. After so long, they were little more than crank calls really, and Norah hated these intrusions into her new life. The man was a nightmare she wanted to forget.

Now residing in the mews, she began calling herself Mrs. Callingham, which of course irritated the real Mrs. Callingham no end. Though he didn't know the full depth of their former engagement, Clement too was getting angry about Vacher's constant overtures. Norah was caught betwixt it all. One day, Clement announced that he'd had enough – he and she were moving to the country.

He had bought a mock-Tudor Edwardian mansion in Pinkney's Green, a village outside Maidenhead. Clement called the house 'Baddow' on account of having been born in Great Baddow, Essex. Driving Norah to it in his Rolls Royce he introduced her to the household staff as Mrs. Callingham. Norah could not hide her amusement as the servants had already worked the situation out. Clement was fourteen years older than Norah and the attractive young 'wife' did not take too much accounting for in their love nest. Norah sensed the resentment and felt that the staff all looked down on her.

Vacher, meanwhile, tracked Norah down to Baddow and resumed his relentless campaign to win her back. He rang and asked to speak to Norah Turner. The housemaid who answered said they had no domestic servants of that name here and hung up. Of course, she and everyone else knew who Norah Turner was – why should they bow and scrape to her when the real Mrs Callingham was in London?

Clement too felt awkward. Deeply religious, he could not ignore how he was committing a mortal sin. The situation was at complete odds with his strong beliefs. Yet he could not find the strength for it to be otherwise. Meanwhile, Norah waited patiently for Clement to divorce Pamela, when all would be above board. Then life took another twist and the great sorrow it caused made her re-evaluate her feelings towards Clement and his religious beliefs.

Norah had always expected that Pamela would cite her in any divorce petition and she was not to be disappointed. To be cited in a divorce carried great stigma in the 1930s, but Norah was carrying a far bigger burden than that. She was pregnant with Clement's baby, a child she claims to have desperately wanted while knowing that Clement would not, for in the terms of the day it would be born a bastard. She pleaded with Clement, but this man of religion told her in no uncertain terms: 'Lose the baby or lose me.' As she saw it, that left her with no choice. Had Norah kept the baby she would have been on her own, an unmarried mother with no support and war with Germany looking certain. He would arrange an abortion in London for her. With loathing for herself and guilt at her actions, she ceded to Clement's wishes.

Clement being Clement, the abortionist turned out to be of the back-street variety in London's East End, all to save money. The scene greeting Norah was horrifying. On arrival, the door was opened by a toothless old hag with a dirty bloodstained apron wrapped around her waist.

'Come in dear,' she trilled.

The woman produced two large hatpins ready to do the dreadful deed. Had Norah been in such a position before? Quite possibly, maybe even probably. But the enormity of what she was about to do amid all that squalor caused her to flee in floods of tears anyway. She returned to Baddow and told Clement that she could not kill their baby.

'Please can we keep it?' she pleaded.

'No,' he replied. 'I'm not divorced yet, you are cited in my wife's divorce papers and you are pregnant. Don't be a fool Norah, lose it.' The man was implacable.

And so, at huge expense this time, Norah was whisked away to Harley Street, where trained medical staff in clean and sterile surroundings put her under anaesthetic. She then awoke without her baby but under a dead weight of shame at the loss. She believed she had done wrong and returned to Baddow to recover her fragile mental state. Yet again she had been let down by a man, the only compensation this time being that he was also disgustingly rich.

Norah always believed that wealthy people ought to

spend their money and preferably on her. Clement however did not agree with that idiom, careful and conservative when opening his wallet. She considered him a miser and her resentment grew. To pay for his two wives Clement was often away working, when Norah would read the Society pages. Sometimes there would be a piece about Pamela giving a glittering party with Noël Coward or the Duke of Gloucester in attendance, while Norah sat isolated in Pinkney's Green. With no money or baby and Paul Vacher constantly ringing her nerves were at breaking point. She would question how Clement could allow her to commit such a terrible act. How could he believe in God but be party to the killing of one of his creatures? She had done all this to protect the good name of the Callinghams, yet wasn't even one of them yet.

Norah decided that she had to do something about the Paul Vacher situation though. If she could rid herself of one problem it might help, so she contacted an old friend to help her – Judge Cecil Whiteley, her former sugar daddy, one of the country's most eminent judges and the Master of Laws.

Cecil sent Vacher a letter telling him to desist and leave Norah alone. The letter did the trick. The phone fell silent and the mail and cables stopped. Norah breathed a sigh of relief. But many years later she was to learn that Paul Vacher had been destined to take his own life in the basement of another Queen's Hotel, this time in Leeds, leaving a widow and son.

In 1938, meanwhile, Norah felt calmer now, though she still had issues, one of the main ones being money. Pamela was living a lavish and decadent lifestyle, paid for by Clement, while she only had her savings, spent on running Baddow and even paying the staff, pawning most of the jewellery given to her over the years at the Café de Paris in the process. All this culminated in a huge argument over an unpaid bill that Clement refused to pay – the final straw.

'Millionaires are not meant to be mean,' she screamed. 'I've done everything for you, Clement Callingham, even killed our baby, and you can't even pay the bloody grocer. I'm leaving you and going back to London.'

Rattled by the outburst, Clement managed to talk Norah around and put his hand in his pocket. It was a tactic Norah would use regularly in the years to come. Threatening to leave usually paid dividends. It kept the husband in his place and a little gift would duly arrive too, with everything made up in the bedroom.

However the rows continued. Clement's mantra was that money was for keeping, not for spending. One luxury he did allow Norah was a new Daimler, the brand she would ultimately become associated with for decades ahead.

And then she fell pregnant again.

***

NOT FOR THE FIRST TIME, Oscar Wilde put it best, on this occasion in *The Importance of Being Earnest*: 'To lose one parent may be regarded as a misfortune; to lose both looks like carelessness.' The same surely goes for the other way around.

Once again, Norah knew there would be no support from Clement as his divorce from Pamela was still not final. However she could not and would not fall at the last hurdle.

It was clear, in her mind, that she needed to facilitate this abortion herself, though the idea of doing so filled her with fright. She saw Clement's views on God and religion as tosh but knew he would not change them so what option did she have? Problem was, she had no money and could not take the backstreet route again. The terrifying hag there still gave her nightmares ... that bloodstained apron ... those clinking hatpins ... she'd wake screaming and soaked in sweat.

Norah longed for the day she could have a child in wedlock, she claimed to adore children and babies. As a valid prospect, it seemed a long way off. She could ask Clement for the further £100 she now needed to pay a second Harley Street bill. Neither could she return to the East End. She could ask Cecil, perhaps, but if this got back to Clement he would suspect Cecil was the father and their relationship would be over. There was no more jewellery from her Café de Paris days to pawn in Holborn, where they were always happy to see Miss Turner ... bracelets ... watches ... rings ... a stunning emerald and diamond brooch with an emerald as large as a Brazil nut given her by a Russian prince who said it had been the property of Tzars. All gone. However she knew the treasure trove would come back tenfold when she became the real Mrs. Callingham.

She wracked her mind thinking she could perhaps do a few nights back at the Café de Paris. It was a pipe dream. Clement would never allow it and she could not risk him getting wind of her plans. Everything would end if he knew.

She still had a crocodile skin case bought for her by an unknown gentleman of title in Asprey, iconic supplier of crowns, coronets and sceptres for royal families around the world. The case was fitted out with silver and enamel bottles and jars. When her gentleman friend purchased it, it had cost two hundred guineas, so Norah thought she must be able to raise hundreds of pounds for the thing. She telephoned the pawnbroker and described the case in detail to him. His gruff response was: 'Five pounds. No call for them, my dear.'

Slamming down the receiver, she then remembered a little trinket on her bedside table. It was a divine little Cartier travel clock, its jade face studded with diamonds in star motifs in a red maroon leather case. She also recalled the dance partner who had given her this beautiful gift, though not, alas, his name. Charles something was the closest she could get, a rather fat second generation Bradford mill owner with a textile empire in the North of England and a dowdy wife sat at home in a brass castle, all turrets and mansard roofs typical of the woollen gentry's homes.

Charles had liked dancing, eating and spending on a huge scale. His big weakness was hostesses and showgirls – he planned to produce a West End show with his favourites as stars! Charles drove around his mills in Bradford in a gold-plated Rolls Royce, a brash show of opulence that Norah would claim as her own a few years down the line.

Norah wrapped the clock in her handkerchief, slipped it into her purse and, thanking God and Charlie, drove her car to the station where she boarded the next train to London and then the shop in Holborn by taxi.

'Miss Turner, how lovely to see you again,' said the pawnbroker as she entered his grimy lair, with its interior of mahogany cases crammed with silver, teapots, trays and salvers. Flat counter cases were crammed with a glittering array of pins and such that twinkled in the dim light. 'What delights do you have for me?, he said, fiddling with the gold Albert chain that hung across his stomach. 'I must have had every deb in town here this month. Very busy, very busy..."

Norah saw this for what it was, an attempt to get her price down. She unwrapped her handkerchief and placed the beautiful timepiece on the counter as his beady eyes lit up. 'Nice, Miss Turner, very nice,' he said, in hushed tones. He then got his eyeglass out and checked the item over to make sure there was no damage or that no little diamonds had come adrift in Norah's bag. 'Thirty pounds, Miss Turner.'

Norah shot back. 'Now please, Mr. Taylor, let's not be silly. If I don't get one hundred and fifty pounds I'm taking it home. It's just too divine to just give away.'

Mr Taylor recoiled as though shot by a silver bullet. 'Never in my life have I paid that sort of price for one of these clocks,' he said.

So Norah scooped it up, dropped it back in her purse and turned on her heels. 'Cash or cheque?' the Pawnbroker enquired just as she reached the door.

'Cash please, Mr. Taylor,' she said.

Whereupon, armed with hard cash, Norah hailed another cab to the one part of Mayfair that held unhappy memories – Harley Street. She entered the clinic with both trepidation and relief. She didn't want to be here but had to be, that was that. She dug out her £100 and booked herself in for a second termination the following day.

Clement was away on business so the timing could not have been better. If anybody saw her, she would complain of a heavy period. Afterwards, with no support, she again felt degraded and bereft of the babies she'd desperately wanted.

Returning to Baddow, she locked herself in her room and cried for days on end, mentally distressed. Her loneliness and pain were all she had for company. The heavy brocade curtains were closed to the world and she took meals in her room asking servants to leave the tray outside. After a while, those tears stopped and upset turned to anger at Clement and his ridiculous religious beliefs. Like all men he was happy to enjoy the sins of the flesh but not their consequences. What hypocrites all men were. Animals was now Norah's opinion.

One bright morning, the maid knocked on Norah's bedroom door. 'Please may I bring in the breakfast tray Mrs. Callingham?' she asked. Norah had started to feel better and the servants' previous contempt for her had now turned to concern. Whatever was up with their usually sassy mistress?

'Yes,' Norah replied.

The maid had barely laid the silver tray on the satin

counterpane when the door flung open. It was Clement, back from work and beaming from ear to ear. He dismissed the maid and sat beside Norah, now propped up in bed, her shoulders covered in a delicate bed jacket trimmed with swans' down. 'I'm free darling! My divorce is absolute! Will you marry me, Norah?'

'Yes, darling,' she replied, her eyes welling with tears of joy. 'Of course I will, yes.'

She could now put all the pain and hurt behind her. Clement fumbled around in his pockets and produced a tiny box. On bended knee, he opened it to reveal a ring with one huge sapphire surrounded by many glittering diamonds.

For once, Norah was lost for words.

***

QUICKLY AND WITHOUT FUSS THE couple booked Chelsea Registry Office, where the newlywed and legal Mrs. Callingham could leave her torments behind.

Finally, she had bagged her millionaire, making everything so much easier to bear.

Clement whisked his bride off on a honeymoon cruise to Trinidad, though Norah later discovered it had been partly paid for by Henekeys as part of a drive to import cigars into their wine houses. How typical!

Norah knew Clement's split from Pamela had cost him a fortune, but he was still a millionaire and she wanted him to loosen those purse strings. Love is all very well but it doesn't pay for diamonds and pearls, Norah would muse.

Nevertheless, after the pain of Norah's abortions and Clement's bitter divorce, things were looking up. Clement had a boat and they enjoyed weekends on the Solent or might take a drive in one of three cars, his beloved Rolls, Norah's

Daimler and a rather racy Ford V8. The servants at Baddow increasingly accepted her, treated the couple with care and respect. And it was during this relative period of calm that Norah fell pregnant again and knew that this third time she would be able to keep the baby she so desperately wanted.

Clement too was thrilled. He had longed for a baby born in wedlock. And in 1939, Norah gave birth to a healthy boy, Lance, named after the only child of Woolworth heiress Barbara Hutton, whom Norah admired and read about daily in newspapers and magazines. Hutton was famed for a large wardrobe made by the leading couture houses and possessed one of the world's most spectacular jewellery collections. Norah was also taken with her dashing Danish husband, Count Kurt von Haugwitz-Hardenberg-Reventlow, the trio living in a London mansion,Winfield House, later gifted to the American government and today serving as the official residence for the Ambassador to the Court of St. James.

In thrall to such role models as ever, Norah yearned for Clement to spend a little more freely on her. The epitome of high maintenance, she too wanted jewels and furs, antiques, fine homes and stunning outfits, but that just was not Clements' style. To him, showing off ones wealth was vulgar and ostentatious. Yet now she had delivered Clement a happy family life, so Norah planned a lavish christening party to make all heads turn. The social hierarchy would be climbed.

The date was set for 23 June 1939, her own birthday. Clement thought he had talked Norah into a more subdued and traditional country affair, the christening to be taken by renowned Dr. Nairn, a well-respected Greek churchman and scholar. His wife, though, invited three hundred guests from the gentry and big business to wet the baby's head.

Norah's taste for the lavish and gaudy was on show. A huge marquee was erected on Baddow's elegant lawn, with five hundred bottles of the finest vintage champagne drunk in the sweltering heat of a glorious summer's day. It helped that Clement was a wine merchant, but guests marvelled at such extravagance. A quartet of chefs brought out a huge silver platter of ham, on one side of which was carved a life-size portrait of baby Lance's mother, her face glistening with gelatine. Who would not gasp and guffaw at that? Clement gawped in disbelief but Norah was the centre of attention, exactly where she loved to be, and centre-stage was where she would remain for decades to come.

Her son's christening gifts ranged from the simple to lavish. From Norah and Clement themselves there was a huge diamond spray brooch which dazzled in the sunshine. Norah was rebuilding her jewellery collection, not yet in the league of Miss Hutton but '...give me time,' she said. Slowly and inevitably Clement was being persuaded to loosen those purse strings and he next agreed that they should take a little holiday in Cannes and Monaco. Norah loved the latter's Casino de Monte-Carlo, with its Belle Époque glamour and gambling buzz. In rooms decorated in gilt and gold, fortunes were won and lost at its tables. Her husband wasn't so keen.

The writer Somerset Maugham called Monte Carlo a 'sunny place occupied by shady people'. When Clement quoted him to Norah she would retort: '...and what would he bloody know?' Norah adored the opulence. 'If it's good enough for the Vanderbilts, Rothschilds and Babs Hutton, it's good enough for Norah Callingham,' was how she saw it.

The timing of their trip to the principality was however unfortunate. War was by now clearly rumbling, although Norah had continued to believe that, shielded by wealth and social status, it would not affect her. Clement, however, had been informed by a friend in the diplomatic corps that war was about to be declared and, on 1 September 1939, it was.

The inconvenience of it! Norah fumed that this jumped up little nobody Hitler had ruined a holiday she desperately needed. No more shopping or gambling, she was fuming. While Norah ranted, Clement quickly loaded his family and their belongings into the Rolls, driving through the night to reach Normandy and the port of Dieppe. The Callinghams, with Louis Vuitton suitcases and trunks piled high, were the last vehicle on, bound for England. Many travellers were left stranded, abandoning cars and luggage in a last ditch attempt to board the vessel. Clement had greased the right palms.

Norah had an intelligent husband with connections. He was well aware what war would mean for the nation if it went on for any length of time. His wife, on the other hand, felt hostilities would end quickly, enabling her to resume her life of spending and fun. Even so, she didn't take much persuading when Clement, like so many people of wealth and power, decided that she, baby Lance, Norah's mother and a nanny should see it all out in America. Knowing large houses would be requisitioned for the war effort, he swiftly sold Baddow and bought a small cottage for himself. When it was safe to do so, Norah and the family would return and he would purchase a lovely new house for them all.

So while the rest of the nation was enduring nightmares about bombs, bullets and air raids, Norah began dreaming of cocktail parties in Palm Beach or life at the New York Plaza where American gentlemen, she knew, preferred blondes. But upon telling an old acquaintance how excited she was to be going, the reaction was one of horror not admiration.

'That's terrible! You can't leave!' the friend exclaimed.

'But Babs Hutton has gone back,' Norah reasoned.

'The Royal Family are staying,' her friend replied, 'and so should you. Shame on you, Norah.'

The exchange had its effect. The wannabe socialite told

Clement to cancel the passages, the smaller abode would be fine. 'Let's drink for victory, King and Queen, Mr. Churchill and the little princess,' she announced, unabashed by the change of heart. And completed the turnaround by declaring: 'The Callinghams are staying! Up yours, Herr Hitler!'

***

CLEMENT HAD SERVED IN THE 1914-1918 war with the King's Royal Rifles Corps. Older now, he enlisted for Home Guard duties and was given the rank of Sergeant. Norah was furious with the 'slight'. She felt his rank should have been the same as in the Great War – Major – but her husband was just happy to do his bit.

Norah mulled over what she could contribute to the war effort. Becoming a land army girl was out of the question, obviously. Neither could she work in a munitions factory – the heat and grime would ruin her hair and complexion. So after careful consideration she enlisted in the Mechanised Transport Corps where the uniform was rather smart she felt, though the stockings were thick and abrasive. Undeterred, she dyed her own silks khaki and no one was any the wiser.

Before enlisting, Norah had to face an examining board, a procedure at which there was a nasty altercation. On being asked how many potatoes there were in a hundred-weight sack she retorted: 'I'm here to fight a bloody war, not count bloody spuds,' believing the paper to be beneath her. The board were shocked by Norah's sassy response but, as one dowdy member pointed out, Mrs. Callingham had her own vehicle which could prove most useful.

The commanding officer was a lady with whom Norah was acquainted from the local Maidenhead Golf Club. Given her complete inability to follow even the simplest of orders, however, the poor woman faced a constant uphill battle. Norah told everyone that the officer was a lousy golfer and even worse at running the corps. Had it not been a voluntary unit, she would have been court-martialled for lack of respect and belligerence. Norah's contempt for social 'superiors' manifested itself throughout her life. Advice was taken as a personal affront. Hurt and petulant, she would please herself and everyone else could mind their own business.

Yet for some reason that nobody could work out – her husband's connections perhaps – she was promoted to run a corps called the Queen's Messengers. Then again, since that corps consisted only of a fleet of Bedford trucks, perhaps she had been given the role as a way to shut her up.

The role was to dispense relief in heavily-bombed areas, usually cities, supplies for the thousands of people who had been bombed out of their homes, lives decimated by the German Luftwaffe. Norah found their plight distressing. She felt real sympathy for the children and old people involved and often thought about little Lance, safe in the countryside while burnt rubble, destruction and death was all around. In fact, such adversity meeting with stoicism on a daily basis humbled Norah. The selfish and indulgent lifestyle took a backseat while compassion for fellow human beings came to the fore. She wept every night to Clement, sharing tales of pain and suffering etched on the faces of orphaned children, sparking arguments over his religious beliefs.

'How could God allow this evil?' she would say.

Against a backdrop of enormous tragedy and suffering, no doubt Norah's own past heartbreaks weighed heavily on her mind. It also inspired bravery. Many areas were cordoned off due to unexploded bombs. If Norah heard a noise or cry of a child, someone shouting for help, she would not think twice about going into the danger area to help, even if that meant risking her own life. Going over the danger line in Bath one time, virtually reduced to rubble, Norah heard sobbing. She saved a child but was then relieved of her duties. Norah would henceforth suffer vivid nightmares that never left her.

Frequently lambasted for her vagaries and frivolity, the one area in which no criticism could stick was in Norah's attitude towards human life and the suffering of others. She was always the first person to help a friend in need whatever the situation, sometimes at great personal hardship.

Having left the Queen's Messengers, Norah could often be seen heading off to blitzed cities voluntarily. Armed with the finest brandy and port from Henekey's cellars, she sought no reward for these efforts, just felt compelled to help people by sharing a little nip and maybe even a sing-song. Everyone looked out for the fine lady coming. She brought a smile to their faces and would tell them all that the war would soon be over and that they would all build their lives again.

In terms of Norah's future public persona, these were formative moments. Those she helped began to know her as 'the guardian angel' and even when, in future years, she was considered 'the dazzling Lady Docker,' there was never any doubt that working class folk were her type of people. They loved her brash vulgarities and she loved them for loving her. She chatted and had sly fags with factory girls and got down on the pavement to play marbles with street kids.

The war, though, continued and for Clement this was not good. At his wit's end, he demanded his wilful and obstinate wife stay at home and stop her dangerous mercy trips. And when a German bomb landed yards from their pretty cramped cottage, he put his foot down. Enough was enough. Though Clement stayed on and ran what was left of the Henekey's business, his family was evacuated to the relative safety of Wales.

The company was by now reduced to just a handful of staff and very little stock as Norah had dispensed most of it. Worse, tragedy then struck Clement when his 20-year-old son, Guy, by his marriage to Pamela, died at Arnhem having been caught by friendly fire, mistaken for a German soldier. Clement's misery was compounded when, weeks later, his beloved brother Lawrence was also killed in action.

This double tragedy broke Clement and his grief took over. He found it difficult to cope with daily life and Norah rushed back from Wales to support him in his hour of need.

Meanwhile, the war staggered on to its conclusion and the whole family were reunited. In 1945, Norah, in typical fashion, urged Clement to splash out on a penthouse flat in Sandbanks, Bournemouth; as today, an enclave on the south coast favoured by the newly wealthy. Clement's burden of grief though was immense. He took to his bed and remained there for weeks with little interest in seeing anyone.

Norah tried to lift his spirits but very little could bring a smile to Clement's sad face. Even Lance, his only son now, could barely draw a smile from a doting father struggling with laboured breathing. The patient was also diagnosed with severe indigestion and thrombosis and moved into a private hospital where, soon after in July, he passed away.

The shock was immense. Norah's life came crashing down. She had wanted a happy ending with the man she loved and her beloved child. Yet instead of celebrating the end of the war with her husband, she reeled from his loss.

The days following Clement's death were a nightmare. She could not comprehend that he had gone and admits in her autobiography that she contemplated taking her own life. Yet, heavily sedated, she did not want to burden Lance with the stigma she had endured with her father. Norah felt lonely and isolated, only love for her child made her carry on.

The Dazzling Lady Docker

Days were long, lasting forever. Nothing interested her, not even spending money. It was an era in which everything was rationed but if you knew the right people anything could be obtained. Norah was numb, her husband dead and buried. She believed her life was over, staring out across Sandbanks in her penthouse eyrie, when one day her maid entered the drawing room as Norah gazed out of the window.

'There is a gentleman to see you, ma'am.'

'To see me?'

"Yes, ma'am. This is his calling card.'

The timid girl handed Norah a small silver salver. Upon it lay an ivory coloured card emblazoned with the name Sir William Collins in gold lettering.

Wilkie, to his friends, was chairman of Cerebos Salt, a multi-millionaire. Norah had met the man a couple of times but could barely remember him. She asked her maid to bring the businessman to the dining room and offered him sherry. He and Norah talked politely about her late husband and the war and Lance and all the things that she and Clement had planned to do before his untimely demise. Wilkie proved a good listener and consoled Norah.

'The world will change for the better now that the war is over,' he said.

The pair exchanged pleasantries and she thanked him for paying his kind and thoughtful respects.

The following day, Norah left for a break in Scotland, the beautiful tranquil scenery would be exactly the tonic she needed. All those lochs and mountains would help her forget. Yet on her return to Sandbanks, days later, there came a hand-delivered letter inviting both Lance and herself to a weekend visit to Sir William's country estate.

Enter husband number two...

9

•

The Salt King

IF NORAH CONSIDERED CLEMENT CALLINGHAM rich,
self-made Sir William Collins was in a whole different league.

Cerebos Salt was a household brand, earning 'Wilkie'
his nickname: 'The Salt King'. His company also controlled
prestigious Fortnum & Mason in London's Piccadilly, oldest
department store in the UK having been established by a
humble footman of the royal court, William Fortnum, during
the reign of Queen Anne in 1707.

Anne, last of the Stuart monarchs and first sovereign of
Great Britain, demanded that her palaces should have new
candles every night. Enterprising William Fortnum collected
the half-used wax and recycled them, using the profits to
create his eponymous corner shop, as it stayed for hundreds
of years before a clutch of royal warrants upped its status
with the English nobility. Sir William Collins loved the story
of how Fortnum & Mason was founded. He doubtless saw

himself in it – not a glimmer of a silver spoon in sight, just hard graft and business acumen. This was a man who began his working life at the tender age of twelve, having ditched school in favour of loading salt on wagons for a few shillings a week. Years hence, if quizzed about his education, he would tell those who dared ask that he'd attended the minor public school, Clifton College, a well-rehearsed falsehood.

What Sir William lacked in education he more than made up for in self-sufficiency. Quickly moving up the ladder at Cerebos he was made a travelling salesman in areas where the company struggled to sell and began to turn them into high earners with impressive figures to match.

From the sales force he went into management. Tricky times? Sales flagging? Never fear, Sir William is on hand to steer us back into calmer – and more profitable – waters. He was elevated from managerial post to the board of directors and in time emerged as chairman of the board. As chairman, he achieved huge dividends for shareholders and himself.

Sir William's biggest business coup was taking control of the company owning Fortnum & Mason. He held a number of directorships – firms were keen to have the astute and hard-working Salt King on their board. In addition to the trophy asset of such a well-known store, he added enviable real estate including a pair of country parks of four thousand acres. In one, every window of the principal dwelling looked over prime Hampshire farmland. The other, Wrexham Park, near Stoke Poges, was a modest sixteen-bedroom Georgian mansion, adjacent to which was a climate-controlled garage housing fifteen cars, including top of the range Bentleys and Rolls Royces. A team of men were employed simply to polish and clean them on the off-chance Sir William might use one.

Other passions were art and antiques, both country homes filled with paintings, ceramics and silverware of the finest quality. In the dining rooms, huge Georgian silver salt cellars sat on the table, piled high with Cerebos salt. And at every meal lashings of salt were piled on every plate. Like the Victorians, Wilkie thought salt the elixir of life. Well it had certainly changed his.

It was to Wrexham Park that the young widow and her boy arrived to spend the weekend. Norah was stunned by its opulence. She could not believe that Sir William lived in this Ducal manor. Baddow had been large but compared to this place it seemed positively suburban.

The household staff numbered sixteen, attentive to guests in every detail, everything of the finest quality. Food and wine was freely available, no sign of wartime rationing. Every bedroom had en suite bathroom facilities, very modern for 1940s England. Bed linen was finest Egyptian cotton and dressing tables groaned with silver jars and bottles filled with creams and colognes from, naturally, Fortnum & Mason.

Sir William could not bear to see a dead flower, so the vast arrangements that adorned every room were checked daily to ensure nothing offended his eye. Norah felt like the country cousin amid such splendour. She knew no-one who lived like it, not even her old flame the Duke of Marlborough. He merely had two rooms at Blenheim Palace.

Like the Duke, though, Sir William was in every way an autocrat. He was aloof and regal, a man of bearing. He ran his private life like his business – with an iron hold. Some saw it as overbearing, over-compensation for a lowly background.

Norah admired Sir William's power and it goes without saying was attracted to his wealth and all that went with it. Slim and tanned with a receding hairline, Sir William had piercing blue eyes that were magnified by thick tortoise shell glasses. He had the look of an elderly bald owl that, sadly, Norah did not find in the least attractive. Still, that money.

The Dazzling Lady Docker

Nobody could ever really tell what was going on behind those spectacles. Sir William gave nothing away in his manner. He was also considerably older than Norah, seventy years old when she had just turned forty.

Sir William was also a widower having lost his wife, Nancy, a few years earlier. He may have been rolling in it, but he was lonely and isolated by his financial resources, in need of a companion though, like Norah wary of gold diggers. They had both worked hard for their respective funds and did not wish to share them with a person of no means.

At first, given the age difference, Norah thought Sir William would be ideal for her mother, Amy. It was a notion she soon put out of her head. Norah, Lance and sometimes Amy became a regular feature at both of Sir William's estates, enjoying upper-class sporting pursuits like shooting parties; Sir William was a fine shot with guns custom made by James Purdy & Sons. Sir William and Norah enjoyed walks together around his beautifully manicured grounds. Norah liked the country life – as long as it was within driving distance of the bright lights of London. And so the gentle friendship of the lonely and rich widower and widow progressed. Norah had no idea Sir William harboured romantic thoughts.

Then, one day, they were sitting in the handsome oak panelled library at Wrexham Park, Norah reading a piece in the newspaper that was of particular interest. 'Forty-nine millionaires from Texas are coming on a visit to England looking for wives!' she read aloud. Then, peering over the top of the paper in question, added. tongue in cheek,: 'If I can't land one of those my name is not Norah Callingham.'

She was shocked by Sir William's response. 'And why would you want to do that,' he asked her, 'when there is one millionaire sitting right here? Why don't you marry me?'

Norah was lost for words, but Sir William went on: 'I

know my age is a concern for you and you may never truly love me like a wife loves a husband, but surely we could be happy? We can live here with Lance and you can be my hostess. It could work, Norah. I would ask nothing of you.'

Norah's killer instinct kicked in. Quickly dispelling any ideas of a match for her mother, she accepted there and then. Here was an elderly gentleman of huge wealth whom she had not had to fight to win an offer of marriage. It had taken her years to land her first millionaire, Clement. Just months after his death, a second was there for the taking.

'Yes,' she said. 'Oh, yes.'

Days later, a diamond solitaire ring arrived from a leading Bond Street jeweller and Norah slipped the rock onto her engagement finger. Like her literary heroine Lorelei Lee, Norah could assess a diamond in seconds. Colour ... clarity ... weight ... calculated before it passed the knuckle. This one was in the region of five carats, she reckoned. It had a fancy yellow colour in a brilliant cut. 'Divine!' she squealed.

But Sir William just stared, first at the ring and then at his bride-to-be. 'Remove it,' he demanded. 'It's yellow.'

'Wilkie darling, it's meant to be,' Norah pleaded. 'It's what they call a "fancy yellow".'

'Well I loathe it,' Sir William thundered. 'It's going back. Take it off now.'

Norah slid the impressive jewel off at his command, only to then hurl it back to Sir William while stamping her feet in anger. Tears of frustration rolled down her cheeks.

'I've got another in my pocket for you darling,' said Sir William.

Norah was aware that men with wealth like Sir William could be mean when buying a girl diamonds. She had seen it many times at the Café de Paris. Sir William fumbled in his blazer pocket. He pulled out a ring and with great dexterity flipped it to Norah. 'I don't want your ring,' she shrieked. 'I bet it's some pinprick of stone. You're so mean, how can you treat me like this?'

Sir William laughed out loud.

'Don't you bloody laugh at me, you cruel and heartless man.'

It was true he had goaded Norah's tantrum. Walking over, he picked up the second ring, held her firmly and slipped it on her finger, a magnificent sight. It was a square cut diamond of at least six carats, brilliant white, shining with an intense light. Norah knew this ring put Sir William's first offering into something from a lucky dip. Her tears of anger turned to tears of joy. Her tantrum was forgotten.

Sir William smiled. He told Norah it had been his late wife's and he had been unsure if he should give it to her. When he saw the first ring, he knew it was meant for her.

'It's the most divine ring I've ever seen,' Norah said. 'I love it Wilkie and will never take it off.'

Amy, however, was strongly opposed to her daughter's union with a man thirty years her senior. 'He's old enough to be your father,' she told Norah, knowing nothing of her earlier plan to make him her stepfather!

Norah sat her mother down and gave her some hard truths about the state of her financial affairs. Clement was rich. He had left Norah the large sum of one hundred and seventy-five thousand pounds, around five million in today's money, but his sudden death had caught them unawares. They had made no provision for any duties on Clement's estate and the Labour government of his namesake, Clement Atlee, had just swept to power, voters having kicked wartime hero Winston Churchill out of the Prime Minister's job. The war had ravaged economy and country.

Atlee was not interested in the rich. He believed they

could look after themselves. He needed cash to pay for the reconstruction of towns and cities, along with social reform. The rich must be taxed for every penny possible. One policy he introduced was death duty at 65 per cent in the pound.

Vast swathes of land were sold off as landowners were faced with these huge tax bills, post-war. Times had changed. Large houses were closing, extensive grounds and parklands were destroyed by mining or building. Woodlands were cut down and art treasures were sold off to pay for it all.

Norah explained to Amy that the Henekey's estate was held in trust for Lance but that she was paying a staggering ninety-eight per cent tax on her cash and investments. 'Mr Atlee is running through my money quicker than I could!' she joked. If she was not careful, there would be little left to support the family.

Amy, like Norah, knew all about life without money and had developed a preference for life with it. She was not prepared to go back to the hovels of back street Birmingham, made much worse by wartime bombs. So she came around to the idea of Norah and Sir William's union very quickly. Not only had he slipped this huge diamond ring on Norah's finger, but a full-length mink coat of the finest pelts costing £8,000 over her shoulders. Money, not poverty, talked.

As for Norah, she made no pretence about marrying Sir William for anything other than cash. She was frank with him too. She needed financial security. He could give her that. He needed a companion. She could provide that. A business deal is what it was, *quid pro quo*.

Yet as their wedding day approached, Norah was to see a side of Sir William she did not like.

It was booked for Caxton Hall registry office, where the guests sat waiting for the bride with Sir William at the front. Norah was a few minutes late, as is the prerogative – indeed requirement – of all brides, but the old gent was becoming increasingly agitated by the wait.

Norah's wedding outfit was to cause more trouble. She had wanted one that would show her in a demure light, a pretty tailored coffee-coloured dress over which was a boxy mink-trimmed jacket, pinned with a diamond brooch.

Norah duly arrived and embarked on her bridal walk only to hear her groom say angrily: 'I told you to wear the brown lace,' fury in his face. Guests looked on as the belittling continued, whispering about the farce unfolding before their eyes. Norah defended herself: 'I didn't wear that as it wasn't new. It would bring bad luck darling.'

'Sentimental tosh,' Sir William bellowed.

The registrar looked on in acute embarrassment while guests shuffled in their seats. Some craned their necks to get a better view, the tension in the room palpable.

Not surprisingly, Norah felt humiliated. Her face had flushed, tears welled in her eyes. She turned on her heels but Sir William placed his hand on her arm to prevent her exit. Guests gasped in horror. Turning back to face the registrar she thought for a second about what Lorelei Lee would do in such a situation? The answer was obvious. She would marry the old sod and take him for everything he had!

And so, in front of a bemused wedding party, Norah Callingham became Lady William Collins. The groom did not kiss his bride. As they left Caxton Hall, it was hardly a match made in heaven. 'She'll salt his tail for that performance!' joked one attendee.

There was, however, still a reception at Claridge's to get through. A chauffeur-driven Rolls Royce was waiting outside to transport the newlyweds there, where more friends and relatives were waiting to greet and toast the happy couple. Norah sank into the luxurious upholstery while Sir William attempted, at last, to kiss his bride, who pushed him away with force. 'I don't think so, Wilkie,' she said in no uncertain tone. That would surely change when her husband reached into the side glove compartment and produced a three-row natural pearl necklace with a diamond clasp. It was stunning though not as stunning as Norah's reaction. If he believed the sight of such an expensive gift would bring his wife around, Sir William was sorely mistaken. As he attempted to place the necklace around Norah's neck, she screamed: 'I don't want them and I don't want you!' and yanked it off, sending pearls cascading around the car like blossom from a tree.

The guests at Claridge's gathered to greet the happy couple did not know that they would arrive at loggerheads. Many looked on in disbelief as the couple on the top table engaged in open warfare. This was not the lavish celebration they had expected.

When the time came for speeches Norah jumped up and made one of her own, speaking of Sir William in sarcastic and condescending tones. She rolled her eyes every time she spoked his name. Sir William's face flushed red. He was livid.

Norah finished her address and swept out of the Art Deco splendour, leaving Wilkie to stew in full view of all. 'Had she got into the waiting Rolls Royce? Had she asked his chauffeur to drive out of London? How soon could she obtain a divorce?' For Norah, the pearl-covered floor of the Rolls could indeed have been 'pearls for tears.'

It was 1946, one year on from Clement's death, and Norah felt utter dismay. Their life together was destined to become one long argument where once there had been a kind and caring companionship. Norah believed Sir William had deep-rooted issues about his humble stock. She also believed that, deep down, he hated women. 'Misogyny is the root of all this,' she told Amy.

Mealtimes were difficult. They sat at opposite ends of a long dining table with Sir William liberally pouring Cerebos salt onto his meals. 'Go on, kill yourself you old fool,' Norah would cackle from the other end. 'Salt is no good for you.'

He would snort back full of contempt for her and pile another spoonful on his food.

***

SIR WILLIAM WAS AN ELEGANT and dignified dresser. His personal appearance and demeanour was impeccable whenever he left his various homes. Only the finest clothing and footwear would do, chosen to reflect the event he would be attending. It was a similar story with his motor cars.

Needless to say he employed a chauffeur, Bale, and a loyal one at that. A fleet of luxury vehicles were emblazoned with their owner's crest: 'SALT SATISFIES.'

Norah, however, had read in an article that the stuff caused hardening of the arteries and high blood pressure, putting a strain on the heart. 'Utter rubbish,' Sir William said. 'It's never done me any harm.'

Wilkie's dignified persona was stretched to its limits one day when his gleaming Rolls stalled in central London. Oxford Street was crowded such a car was an unusual sight. Norah suggested to Bale that they should get out and push. 'I will do no such thing and neither will you,' snorted his boss. 'Do not show me up Norah.'

Meanwhile, the hooting of horns intensified and fellow motorist began getting out of their cars and banging on the windows. 'Come on, move this heap,' one man shouted.

Sir William sat impassive in the back, staring straight ahead, acknowledging nothing or no-one, left or right.

'This is bloody ridiculous, Wilkie,' said Norah, as her

husband impersonated a marble statue. 'We are going to get lynched.' But the statue said not a word. Enough was enough. Norah got out of the car and, with the help of a by-stander, pushed it into a sidestreet while Bale steered. 'I hate this disorganised motoring,' Sir William said, stuck to his seat.

The old chap was however a supporter of good causes. In her book, along with sharing anecdotes such as the one above, Norah called him '...the most charitable man I know.' Before adding: 'Though some charity doesn't begin at home.'

Sir William Collins was patron of many organisation to which he contributed substantial amounts of cash. His largest donation was a cheque for half a million pounds to the Royal College of Surgeons, to aid in their research. His portrait and a bust reside there to this day in honour of his generosity.

Domestically, though, along with his uncomfortable behaviour, Norah detected problems with his health. In short, he was not a well man. He began ignoring servants and staff in his companies, many of whom had served for generations. And rudeness turned to hostility, causing outright distress. 'Never seen you in my life!' he yelled at someone who had worked alongside him for forty years. Norah tried to placate such people but her concerns were shared by Sir William's fellow board members. He was, they felt, unfit to conduct his duties, however the chairman wielded ultimate power.

Sir William grew more and more confused. He would get into his car and tell Bale to drive him to Fortnum & Mason when the board meeting was at Cerebos Salt, or similar.

Norah decided to take matters in hand. She telephoned Jack Weedy, chairman of Cerebos Salt, to warn him of Wilkie's deterioration, only to be informed days later that Sir William had been in fine form at their latest meeting, giving a brilliant and rousing speech. Weeks passed and Norah's homelife was becoming a nightmare. Lance was scared by his stepfather's outbursts and the servants did not know what to make of the sad sight of Sir William losing his mind in front of them. One day he would be on top form as the captain of industry, the Salt King himself. The next he was withdrawn, distant and morose, holding no recollection of his actions in the previous hour let alone day. This was more than ill-tempered ranting.

It got to the stage where he had no idea who his wife was or certainly what she was called. 'Is it Nancy?' he asked a guest at Wrexham Park, having introduced Norah as 'Mrs. Callingham.' He also grew jealous of the attention she gave Lance. In a childlike way, he wanted that.

Nowadays, Sir William would doubtless be diagnosed with senile dementia, Alzheimer's maybe. In 1940s England he was simply losing his marbles.

On one occasion Norah decided to cheer her son up, as he was himself becoming withdrawn and unhappy due to Sir William's behaviour. She had been to London shopping and bought him a shiny Hornby train set. Lance was thrilled with the gift, as any child would be, but his stepfather was livid at this further sign of her preference for the boy. He became very aggressive towards mother and son, to the point where they believed he would do them physical harm. Finally, Norah had reached breaking point so packed her bags and, with Lance and Amy in tow, walked out.

Their destination was Berkshire, where they rented a property in Maidenhead and attempted to settle into sedate and happy family life. For a while it worked. Lance perked up, the trio enjoyed each other's company and began to laugh again, something they hadn't done in a very long time.

Their peace, though, was shattered by a call from Sir William's secretary, who, Norah, believed, had always had it in for her, thinking her an opportunist. In Norah's account, the secretary told her with great delight: 'If you don't return to your husband he will kill you and cut you out of his will.' So she shrieked down the line: 'Tell the old sod I'd rather live in poverty than go back to him,' slamming down the receiver.

His behaviour then became even stranger. After a letter from Sir William's solicitors arrived telling her that she had indeed been cut out of his will – the new beneficiary of a fortune totalling many millions in cash, property, shares and antiques was the aforementioned Jack Weedy of Cerebos Salt, although Norah and Lance would still receive five hundred pounds each! – he then telephoned her out of the blue in a very conciliatory manner. Bright and eager to make amends, he offered her the olive branch of a cruise on the *RMS Queen Elizabeth* to America and so the pair were swiftly reunited.

A romantic happy ending, then? Well, no, obviously. As would have been obvious to anyone with no inheritance in mind – and maybe ought to have been anticipated by Norah herself – elderly Sir William's mental state was as erratic as ever. One day he could be fine, laughing, joking and enjoying himself. The next he shouted and swore at anyone who dared cross his path. Norah bore the brunt of it, though she at least stood to gain from enduring those tirades. Fellow passengers, knowing or caring little for that, looked on in disbelief.

Upon docking in New York, a car transported them to their hotel in midtown Manhattan. Norah was horrified by its shabbiness and, while Sir William took a bath, wasted no time in having the bellboy remove her luggage and call a cab, leaving a scribbled note that read: 'At the Plaza.'

Her husband was furious. Pausing only to get dried, dressed and delivered to said address, he barged into Norah's new opulent suite bellowing: 'Why have you come here?'

'I am not entertaining business associates and guests in a flea pit boarding house,' she replied, as Sir William slumped into a gilded chair decorated in the style of Louis XVI.

The Dazzling Lady Docker

The trip was doomed. One half of the couple often did not know why he was there or who he was. On going out to dinner one evening, he grew disoriented and gashed his head getting out of a car, a wound requiring twelve stitches. Back at the Plaza he took to his bed, while Norah took to Bergdorf Goodman, a luxury goods store on Fifth Avenue. Sir William then developed a fever , in a sorry state. He sat jabbering, his head bandaged, unshaven and dishevelled.

Norah cancelled their engagements, desperate to leave the Big Apple. The only reason she was in the United States at all was because Sir William had led her to believe that he had reinstated her in his will. Then, while packing their cases and looking for passports, she found a copy of the document and, to her horror, read the following words:

> I, Sir William Collins, leave my estate to my dear friend and colleague Jack Weedy. To my wife Norah Collins I leave the sum of five hundred pounds. To Lance Callingham I leave the same. They know why I have left them this amount.

Norah could not believe it and stormed into the bedroom to confront her befuddled husband. 'How could you trick me like this, William? I believed you.' Then she let rip about the injustice he had put her through and began hitting him with rolled-up copy of the *New York Times*. She could take no more. Tears poured down her face as she dealt blow after blow. Sir William's reaction to the assault has gone unrecorded.

On arrival back in England, Norah sought advice from her solicitor. He advised her to get out of the marriage, saying that Sir William leaving her such a small part of his fortune would indicate that she had probably been unfaithful. Norah chose to follow his opinion, the legacy already appeared lost.

When the time came to tell Sir William she was going, Norah said: 'Wilkie, my solicitor is telling me to leave you. I have listened to his legal advice but what I can't understand is your motive for cutting me off virtually penniless. If I came back you said I would be reinstate in your will. You tricked me. Why have you done this? What have I done?'

'Have I?' Sir William asked, suitably confused.

Norah though continued with her diatribe. How cruel and wicked he was. His actions would not only ruin her life but also her reputation. 'They will all think I am a tart,' she wailed as her husband sat impassively.

'I will change it back,' he said once Norah's rant came to an end and he was able to get a word in. And, true to his word, that is exactly what he did, naming his wife as sole beneficiary while ordering his solicitor to draw a new version up. Elated, Norah decided to celebrate by having her hair done only to receive a frantic phone call en route informing her that Sir William had just collapsed and was at death's door in a coma. Worse, he hadn't yet signed the new will.

In her book, Norah insists that she put all her energies into getting Sir William better, as well she might. She hired a team of nurses to attend him round the clock. She consulted a leading Harley Street physician who advised: 'Sir William is a dying man, Lady Collins. You must realise that.' Norah was horrified by such blunt tones, with no care for her and Lance's plight. Just a bleak prognosis of imminent death.

Sir William began hallucinating as his life ebbed away. And Norah had another shock, finding one of her husband's nurses in bed with him. She threw the half-dressed woman out while the nurse screamed: 'You don't love him! I do.'

But then, after a nightmare few days, Sir William came out of his coma. Joy was unconfined, or at least it would have been had he not now believed the errant nurse was his wife.

The Dazzling Lady Docker

Further drama unfolded when Norah was accused of giving her husband sleeping tablets, another nurse having found one in his bedclothes. Sir William's doctor cornered her. 'You take Soneryl, don't you, Lady Collins?'

'Are you accusing me of trying to kill my husband?' she shrieked.

'Well, it doesn't look very good does it,' he replied.

'Don't be so bloody stupid,' she said. 'Sir William is being spoon-fed. How could he take a tablet?'

The inadvertent culprit, it turned out, was her mother, Amy, who took turns with nurses in sitting at Sir William's bedside. While doing so, the pill must have fallen out of her apron, in the pocket of which were large amounts of Soneryl carried on account of her acute hypochondria. Miss Marple would have a field day with that.

Sir William's condition remained serious for months with little change, until one morning a nurse came running: 'Lady Collins, he's awake and calling for you!' Norah ran to his room to find him sitting up in bed as bright as a button, apparently both happy and well. Norah burst into floods of tears. It was a miracle!

'Hello, little girl,' he said, while Norah kissed his face. 'Have I been a pain?'

'No, darling,' Norah said. 'I don't believe you have.'

And then, like the autocrat he was, he dismissed the nurses with a wave of his hand having ordered a full English breakfast. Soon, he would be descending the grand staircase at Wrexham Park, reading the papers and checking the share prices. After a light lunch, he and his wife then walked arm in arm around the estate, Sir William saying to Norah: 'You know, I never did sign that will, did I? Get the butler to call my solicitor. He must be here by six o'clock tonight to witness it.' There was renewed vigour in his voice.

'Let's do it tomorrow, darling,' Norah recalls herself saying. 'It can wait. I don't want you stressed by all that.'

They walked back to the house and Sir William called his close friend Andrew Veitch and two other witnesses – Jack Weedy, about to lose millions of pounds, and Sister Bray, one of the nurses who cared for him. Once everyone was present, he bestowed it all, lock stock and salt cellar, to his wife. After signing with a flourish, he placed the Dunhill fountain pen on his desk and announced: 'I think we all need champagne!'

The sparkle was back, the old man's eyes full of life. He knocked back flute after flute and retired to bed at 10.30pm, telling Norah he didn't want to overdo it on the first day of the rest of his life. Norah kissed him goodnight. 'Goodnight little girl,' he whispered in her ear. 'I love you.'

Those were the last words from Sir William that Norah was to hear. During the night he fell into another coma from which this time he never emerged. Three weeks later he was dead and Norah was widowed for a second time.

In her autobiography, Norah writes that she had grown to love Wilkie while nursing him back to health. Although fabulously wealthy in her own right, she was heartbroken, having believed the couple had turned a corner. Her goal had always been to acquire great wealth, it's true, but she would come to feel lonely and vulnerable with it. For great wealth can cause as many problems as poverty, she found.

The upshot was that Norah was soon on the lookout for a suitable candidate to fill Sir William's immaculately polished shoes. Someone whose wealth exceeded her own, but who was prepared to lavish it upon her. Common sense dictated that she should keep her own fortune safe and spend someone else's. Where might such a man be found?

10

•

Sir Bernard Docker

SIR BERNARD DOCKER WAS AN industrial titan, most famous as chairman of Birmingham Small Arms – B.S.A. – the monolithic company that produced cars, bicycles, arms and ammunitions. Under the B.S.A. umbrella came such global household names as Daimler, Triumph and Sunbeam, the world's largest motorcycle manufacturer.

The arms and munitions division was one of the most profitable subsidiaries and supplied the British Armed forces.

B.S.A. consisted of twenty or so companies strategically acquired to complement each other within the conglomerate. One company made steel or chrome for Daimler, another supplied machine tools for Triumph, while another produced paint for bodyworks, meaning B.S.A. needed no-one else to make component parts for its products. Huge profits stayed within this international goliath of post-war Britain.

Sir Bernard became chairman in 1940, when all B.S.A.

factories worked at full capacity supplying munitions in the fight against Hitler. However Docker family involvement can be traced back to 1906. Sir Bernard's father, Dudley Docker, and brothers laid the foundations of an industrial empire that would equal vast enterprises across the pond. The American fortunes of the Vanderbilts, Harrimans and Rockefellers had also been built on emerging markets, albeit in railroads, steel and oil but with the same model of swallowing up companies to supply their own. Ultimately this was to create monopolies it would take decades to break.

Dudley began his working life in the family law firm, a career he soon knew was unsuitable. In 1881, he threw in the towel and with sibling William founded Docker Brothers, a varnish business, his first step towards the pinnacle.

He also played cricket for Derbyshire, until 1889 when his business interests began to take up all his time and effort. Three years before, another brother, Ludford, had also come on board in what was now a new family business, their father Ralph passing away in 1887 and leaving his three sons a small inheritance. This was invested in their fledgling set-up and it came when it had a desperate need of a capital injection. After which, Docker Brothers began to grow steadily but surely at a pace that really picked up when they moved out of varnish and into the more lucrative paint market.

By 1894 the company had offices in London and, thanks to Dudley's talent for advertising and boardroom prowess, went from strength to strength. It was skill that enabled a deal to be closed that sealed the family fortunes and made the name Docker synonymous with industrial Britain for sixty years. In 1902, Dudley, William and Ludford amalgamated five rolling stock companies into one – the Metropolitan Amalgamated Carriage and Wagon Company, soon to be one of the largest companies in Edwardian Britain.

By 1911, the combined staff totalled fourteen thousand people within a huge factory space of some four hundred and seventy-five acres. And for the past five years Dudley had been a director of B.S.A., then in its infancy, making a small range of motorcycles and bicycles. He grew their fortunes further, developing interests for Dockers in directorships of W&T Avery Ltd, the weighing equipment firm. Just like his American counterparts, he invested heavily in railway companies up and down the country, using their method of cleverly amalgamating lines to cut costs and thereby create more profits. Dudley realised that in a booming economy people would demand greater mobility. He was right. The railways were one of his most lucrative investments.

When the Great War broke out in 1914 the Metropolitan Carriage Company began to produce tanks. Thousands rolled off the production lines, more huge profits the result.

Dudley was also a director of the Midland Bank. He joined the board there in 1912 and would remain an active member until his death in 1944. The position was then offered to Sir Bernard, who continued his father's work.

Dudley had married Lucy Constance Hebbert in 1895 and, on 9 August a year later, Bernard Dudley Frank Docker was born to the doting couple. Bernard would be Dudley and Lucy's only child and they loved and cherished him.

He was born into a life of immense privilege, but also duty. He knew from an early age that he would take over the family's enormous interests. Bernard never shied away from the weighty legacy of an heir apparent. His own drive and ambition would continue to grow the Docker empire.

In 1935 Dudley and Lucy had purchased the beautiful Coleshill House in Amersham, Buckinghamshire. The private estate consisted of a lovely Georgian stucco painted mansion set within extensive manicured gardens and grounds. The couple had longed to leave the industrial grit and grime of Birmingham where even the elite suburbs of Edgbaston were being compromised by the spread of the city.

To complement the Buckinghamshire estate the couple also owned a huge apartment in Berkeley Square, in the heart of Mayfair. Here they entertained the great and good of the day in lavish style.

Of Dudley Docker's many achievements perhaps today he is best remembered for his financial support of Sir Ernest Shackleton's trans-Antarctic expedition of 1914. Shackleton had received a reported ten thousand pounds from the British government, a figure short of that needed. Turning on the charm, the explorer squeezed twenty-four thousand more from Scottish jute baron Sir James Caird, and then persuaded another ten grand from the Docker pocket. The final ten thousand came from philanthropist and tobacco heiress Janet Stancomb-Wills, enabling the purchase and fitting out of *Endurance*, the three-masted barquentine Shackleton wanted for the journey. Each of the donors had a lifeboat named in their honour and, when *Endurance* tragically sank, the crew on Dudley Docker survived. If the British public hadn't heard the name before, they certainly did now. Newspapers were full of the story, earning the Dockers a footnote in history with one of the world's greatest adventurers.

Endurance sank in the winter of 1915 when Britain was at war with Germany and Dudley was at the height of his business success. It was said he had an aptitude for financial affairs that was hard to surpass, a brand of vision unique in Britain, marked by shrewd deals, acquisitions, mergers and takeovers. From its beginnings in the Birmingham varnish trade, it now rivalled companies like Krupp, a centuries old German dynasty, and the multinational Thyssen.

Dudley also put considerable energy into the formation

of the Confederation of British Industry (CBI), still following his policies to today. Respected and feared, he was regarded as a forward-thinking groundbreaker who could get things done while ruthless in ambition for his empire.

Bernard was groomed to replace him from childhood, a prospect that far from filling his son with dread taught him the virtue of patience. The moment came in 1940, as Docker senior stepped down as chairman of B.S.A. and handed cover the reins. However Dudley could never quite leave the stage and continued to be a back-seat presence until his death, aged 81, in July 1944. The bulk of his vast fortune then went to Bernard, although he also left a scholarship fund in the fields of engineering and science to Birmingham University.

Bernard's character was different, less driven. Shy and introverted, people referred to him as a safe pair of hands. Of course, all of that would change with the arrival in his life of Norah, who referred to him as 'Millionaire Number Three.'

If there had been boxes to tick, Sir Bernard Docker would have had a full house. He was single, only ten years older than herself and, most importantly, owned one of the largest fortunes in the country. In fact it was so large that Norah believed it could never be dissipated. There was only one problem – Sir Bernard was not an easy man to catch.

He had been wed before to Jeanne Stuart, a glamorous actress of stage and screen, born Ivy Sweet in Hampstead. After theatre and rep her movie debut came in 1931, two years before the couple were married having crossed paths at a London club. Neither had a clue who the other was but chatted away and shared a dance. The next evening they met again, by which time a waitress had informed Jeanne that this chap, rather plump and nearly forty, was one of the richest men in the country. What more could an actress keen to break into the big time desire? All her powers of seduction were employed to win the shy Bernard, who fell head over heels in love with this beguiling beauty.

The sex siren had snared the multi-millionaire. Quickly they became engaged and after a short engagement married in 1933, to the horror of Bernard's parents. Dudley and Lucy Docker had dreamed he would marry into the landed gentry, combining new money with blue blood and thereby sealing the immense rise from Docker Brothers. They had expected that this romance with a movie starlet was a flash in the pan, so were incredulous at the development, believing Jeanne to be a gold digger out to fleece them of their family fortune.

The pressure from Bernard's parents grew on a daily basis until, eventually, their son capitulated to their wishes and the couple divorced in 1935. As Jeanne left Britain for the United States, Bernard settled a large fortune on her, ensuring she would have no need to rely on the precarious movie industry for cash. He needn't have worried. In America, Jeanne would meet and marry an even bigger fish – Baron Eugène Daniel de Rothschild, member of the fabulously rich banking dynasty and grandson of Salomon Mayer von Rothschild, one of the world's great financiers. That marriage took place in 1952, when Jeanne retired from the silver screen. In reality, her credits were mostly forgettable British affairs and by then her billing had slipped into low budget comedies such as *Old Mother Riley Joins Up* (1939), with Arthur Lucan.

Jeanne and Eugène settled in Monte Carlo, where life in a penthouse apartment decorated with antiques and works of art by Renoir and Picasso suited the new Baroness Jeanne von Rothschild very nicely indeed. Monaco's jetset were a glittering moneyed circle and the von Rothschilds drank and dined with the principality's first family, Prince Rainier and his movie star wife Grace Kelly, plus the Duke and Duchess of Windsor and Jacqueline Kennedy Onassis. The marriage lasted until Eugène's death in 1976, while Jeanne continued to enjoy her life of luxury until her demise in 2003.

Norah detested the woman. She could not bear to have her name mentioned in the same breath as Bernard's. The fact that Jeanne had gone on to marry into the Rothschilds only made that hatred worse. Jeanne's regular appearances in the society pages and best-dressed women lists sent Norah into apoplexies of spite. Jeanne was sleek and sophisticated with an elegant aloofness. Her looks were compared to those of the Hollywood legend Norma Shearer, sultry good looks that afforded her legions of admirers. Her film credentials ensured an entrée to the best parties and society events on both sides of the Atlantic. Norah, meanwhile, had to struggle for her millionaires. It all made Norah venomous.

The idea that Jeanne could have been the first Lady Docker sent Norah doolally. 'There could only be one Lady Docker,' she shrieked at Sir Bernard in argumentative moods. Or, after a few drinks, might say: 'And what did your parents think of your marriage to that harlot?' It was a bold question. One can only imagine that they would not have been any more endeared to Bernard's next wife – a one-time dance hostess with a colourful past, two dead millionaire husbands behind her and hot on the tail of number three.

Another aspect of Jeanne's life that infuriated Norah was how she and the Baron lived in Monaco, a place Norah loved, remember, but which for reasons that will become clear future circumstances dictated she could not enter. Given that the Rothschilds were so friendly with the royal family, it was Jeanne who took the blame for it.

Psychologically, the effect of Sir Bernard's first wife leading such a glamorous lifestyle in Monte Carlo pushed all her insecurity buttons. So she pushed every boundary of restraint in her desire to equal and surpass her. The spending, publicity and craving of attention from Sir Bernard and the media was astonishing. The symbols of the super-rich, the cars, furs, jewels and yachts became ever more important to her, the outward proof of her position that she needed.

It was competitiveness that Norah would vehemently deny, yet her insecurities were deep-rooted. Her father's suicide, near destitution, her days as a dance hostess, the aborting of inconvenient babies in her quest for a millionaire, added up they turned into her into a very complex character. She said to the world : 'Look at me! I am Lady Docker and I am richer than you.' Well, pretty soon she would be Lady Docker, but she would never be richer than Jeanne.

***

NORAH CRAVED ATTENTION FROM ALL who would give it her, from those kids in the streets with whom she played marbles to movie stars and kings. All eyes had to be on her. Sir Bernard however was slightly less enamoured with his future wife's predilection for the limelight.

Sir Bernard had everything Norah needed in a man. He owned a stunning estate, Stockbridge, in Hampshire, and a stylish apartment next door to Claridge's, her favourite hotel. The jewel in the crown was his 65-metre superyacht, *Shemara*.

Since Sir William's death, Norah had been pursued by a number of good looking younger men. She was a sucker for male beauty but experience had taught her that the good looking ones invariably live off their face and wits. Not unlike herself. But now Norah was both wealthy and titled, so the widowed Lady Collins knew she could not afford to make a mistake. And so she took the calculated decision to set her sights firmly on Sir Bernard Docker, a match made in heaven.

Not that the partnership had much, if anything, to do

with romance. Sir Bernard saw it more as a business merger and, however she tiptoed around the idea in her book, you would have to suspect that Norah did too. The two fortunes combined would be among the largest in the country, and the man of the house(s) naturally expected that he would be controlling the purse strings. Naturally, he was wrong.

Barely had Wilkie breathed his last than Norah began working desperately behind the scenes to meet this next and elusive tycoon. She had been a widow for just a few months when a mutual friend provided an entrée at Norah's request, a letter to which Sir Bernard was at a loss to know how to respond. Who was this Lady Collins? He was intrigued but little did he know. Norah's plans were already well laid.

Like a lamb to the slaughter, curious Sir Bernard asked his personal assistant to place a call to the mysterious woman. He invited her to his London apartment in Claridge House, Davies Street, London W1, an invitation Norah was thrilled to receive. Yet she realised she could not go without a good reason. She could hardly turn up and say: 'I want to marry you.' He would have thought her quite mad.

So she concocted an elaborate story that she wished to carry on her late husband's charity work. Like Sir William, Bernard Docker was a prolific and generous donor. 'Would you, Sir Bernard, be able to help me continue the good works that Sir William had put in place..?' was an excellent opening.

So off she went, dressed demurely in a black jersey two-piece suit by Balmain, with a simple string of pearls around her neck. A pearl spray brooch on her lapel finished the look of understated chic. On arrival, she was taken aback by the impressive art deco interiors, although found the clean cool lines a little cold and clinical. Her mind was working hard. A few bits of French furniture, some Dresden figures and a bit of chintz would brighten it up. It needed a woman's touch.

She was ushered into a huge office that, she felt, looked a little like a bank or insurance company and was greeted by Sir Bernard, the man who would change her life forever.

He was friendly and courteous, but also cautious and a little bemused. Norah grew nervous and her well-rehearsed plan began to unravel. The gameplan of charity work chat failed her, she could not get her words out in coherently. So she talked about the weather instead. Then, in a last-ditch attempt to rescue the debacle, she blurted out a lame tale of her sister Alma having known Bernard back in Birmingham.

Sir Bernard sat impassive as Lady Collins babbled. The meeting limped on in unredeemed awkwardness until there was nothing else for Norah to do but take leave. After doing so she went straight into Claridge's next door and ordered a bottle of pink champagne. She felt she had blown it.

Next day, she sent Sir Bernard a card thanking him for taking the time out of his busy business life, then set to work on Plan B. She decided to bombard the hapless tycoon with correspondence. But Bernard merely became even more bemused, his initial caution turning into a feeling that she was ridiculous. In a chance meeting, though, he would give Norah chance to continue her pursuit. By chance, they had both been invited to an informal charity dinner party hosted by Sir Paul Dukes, the famous MI6 agent and author known as the 'Man of a Hundred Faces'.

This time when Norah and Bernard's paths crossed they chatted comfortably. As the evening drew to a close, Sir Bernard offered to walk her home, an offer she accepted. For she had a Plan C up her sleeve – claiming interest in buying a Green Goddess. She had been to the Earls Court Motor Show, she said, and seen the new car, made by Hoopers, a B.S.A. subsidiary. A vehicle was duly delivered in order that Lady Collins might have a test drive.

The chap who brought it was keen to get Norah to sign on the dotted line. He kept telling her what a wonderful car it was, such an exclusive model, mindful of commission. But Norah had no intention of buying the thing and it went back to the salesroom, along with the disappointed salesman.

This and other clues ensured that Sir Bernard had by now got wind of Norah's intentions, her calculated pursuit. Rather than put him off, it piqued his interest. If he was wise and careful, perhaps they could enjoy each other's company. And so under this impression he invited Norah to dinner at Mirabelle in Mayfair. She was beside herself with glee. 'Why yes, of course, I'd be delighted,' she said, breathlessly down the telephone. 'What time?'

'About 7pm. I will have a car collect you.'

Opened in 1936, Mirabelle, in Curzon Street, became one of London's most exclusive restaurants, a haunt of the rich and famous until the 1960s, its fine European cuisine and exclusivity making it a place to be seen. Demolished in 2017, its reputation was briefly revived when owned by celebrity chef Marco Pierre White from 1998-2007 . On that evening in 1948, Norah and Sir Bernard enjoyed a gourmet meal washed down with copious amounts of the very finest fizz.

Which is not to say that their date went with a swing. Norah found Sir Bernard's company a tad dull, boring even. All he talked about was cars and bikes. However, a tycoon he was and the pair continued to see one another regularly. One night they even went to the Café de Paris, where Bernard droned on and his lady friend focussed on that vast fortune. But in time a friendship did begin to grow.

Like all courtesans, Norah had other irons in the fire who she played with along the way to ensure she snared the loot. These included a handsome Swedish businessman met at an embassy dinner who was desperate to marry her. Norah played him off against Sir Bernard to keep her plan moving along, knowing it would bring him running.

She packed her bags and headed to Stockholm to meet her lover's family and announce their engagement. The plan worked. Sir Bernard grew angry then jealous then fretful and upset. In any case, it was a trip dogged with mishaps. Bad weather caused hours of transport delays and by the time she checked into her hotel she was totally exhausted. Just as she was climbing into bed the telephone rang.

'Will you accept a call from London?' the receptionist asked. Her heart leapt. She knew who that would be.

Bernard's worried voice came on the line. 'There you are, at last,' he said, and began to cry. 'Thank god you are safe, where have you been? I've been ringing your hotel all day and night. Darling I've been so worried. Please come back. Our future is together.'

'And what do you think my Swedish boyfriend will say to that?' Norah replied and hung up. So much for Sir Bernard having the upper hand!

As she slipped beneath the bedclothes she knew that other blonde whom gentlemen preferred, Lorelei Lee, and her favourite actress and dancer Peggy Hopkins Joyce would have been proud of her. That's how you catch a millionaire she thought. All she had to do now was to get rid of the decoy of her handsome, rich but utterly manipulated Swedish lover.

The next day she attended her own engagement party and met his family. She talked about how excited she was at the prospect of living in Stockholm and how much she loved Sweden. Then, later that evening, fled the party and went back to her hotel, preparing to depart. The phone rang again. This time it was her Swedish fiancé, angry and bewildered by her rude exit. 'You have acted disgracefully to me and my family,' he yelled.

The Dazzling Lady Docker

Calmly, she apologised and once again hung up. The plan had always been to snare a much bigger fish than this little Swedish herring. The attraction of Sir Bernard was clear for all to see.

With Christmas approaching, Norah invited Bernard to spend the holiday with her, Lance and Amy in Bournemouth. She knew that would test his commitment. How would he respond to Lance? Amy would be easy, fully aware of who Sir Bernard Docker was while being eager to gain such social acceptance. Norah had played a good hand. They all had a lovely Christmas and greatly enjoyed each other's company. Lance was looking for a steady father figure after turbulent years and had Bernard, placid by nature, hanging on to his every word. Here was a caring and kind man who believed that every child needs both parents in his or her upbringing.

The scene was set for Bernard to pop the question and become Norah's third millionaire husband. Amy was in seventh heaven. After all these years she would be a woman of substance in Birmingham, way above those families who had looked down on the Turner family. Amy firmly believed that marriage into the Docker dynasty was the equivalent of marrying into the British Royal family and, for her, it was.

But, as always, the best laid plans have hiccups and Norah could create problems at the best of times.

She and Bernard were invited to a New Year's Eve ball given by Tate & Lyle heir, Lord Leo Lyle, who was also one of Norah's former sugar daddy dance partners during her Café de Paris days. He had always had a soft spot for Norah, a very generous dance partner, showering her with gifts. And now, years later, his New Year's ball was in full swing.

The guests were having a wonderful time. Champagne was flowing as the countdown to 1949 drew nearer. The band began to play an Ivor Novello song that Norah loved, 'We'll

Gather Lilacs'. She had danced to this tune many times and often with Leo Lyle. Now he jumped to his feet, grabbed Norah's hand and took her out onto the dance floor.

'It's our tune, Norah,' he boomed, for all to hear.

'No, Leo. I'm dancing with Bernard,' Norah vigorously asserted. And she did dance to the song in Bernard's arms, though Leo had seriously rattled the industrialist's cage.

The more Norah loved the ball, the more petulant and jealous Bernard grew. Mood swings made him unresponsive, red rag to a bull for his future wife. She hated sulking, found it childlike and uncalled for, so decided to give him a taste of his own medicine. She and Leo Lyle took to the dance floor for real this time and, for the rest of the evening, the two whispered sweet nothings into one another's ear.

'You're not marrying Docker are you, Norah?' Leo said. 'He's not for you. He's an old bore. Darling girl, come with me to South Africa. We will have a ball.'

But Norah was far too clever to be taken in by hollow promises she knew would lead to nothing. He saw her as a good time girl, but Norah had moved on from those Café de Paris days. Nevertheless, Leo was charming, fun and witty, and terrific company compared to the grump in the corner.

Bernard sat, arms folded, watching the revellers. And, shortly before midnight, the radio was tuned to the chimes of Big Ben. All joined hands as the band struck up 'Auld Lang Syne'. 'We'll take a cup of kindness yet,' they sang, but there was one person in the ballroom who felt no kindness towards Norah. Sir Bernard, publically humiliated and cuckolded by Norah's outrageous flirtations, was not amused.

She had overplayed her hand and gone too far.

As they left the party in a chauffeur-driven Rolls Royce in the early hours of January 1, no words were exchanged by the courting couple. Once home, Bernard went to his room.

The Dazzling Lady Docker

Norah banged and slammed doors, but also said nothing. She would never respond to sulking but her catch was in danger of slipping the net, and after all that planning and scheming. In anger, Bernard Docker was more than a match for Norah.

The next morning, Amy bounded into her daughter's bedroom. Norah was fast asleep under a pile of satin covers emblazoned with her monogram, NC, gilded cherubs gazing down upon her slumber. 'Wake up,' Amy hollered. 'He's packing his suitcase. You stupid girl, he's leaving.'

Alarming visions of lost high society flashed before her mother's eyes, but Norah was hungover and told her, in belligerent terms, to let the fellow go. 'What have you done? What happened last night?' Amy was desperate. 'Don't you realise the man loves you? If Bernard leaves this house you will never see him again,' she pleaded.

Norah, though, just scoffed beneath the satin. 'I don't need him, or anyone else for that matter. And you are hardly in a position to tell me about relationships, are you mother?'

A furious Amy turned the table quickly, admonishing Norah like a child. 'You get your dressing gown on madam, and you get up and go and apologise to Bernard – NOW!'

Whenever Amy adopted these tones, Norah took heed. In fact it was about the only time she would do as she was told. Amy's anger jolted her daughter into action. She rose and crept along the landing, set to persuade Bernard to stay.

'Bernard darling, I'm a bloody fool. I'm truly sorry about last night and carrying on the way I did.' Norah put full effort into her words. 'Look at me, my hair's a mess, I've got no make-up on and I'm in my nightie. But I love you.'

Bernard stopped packing and sat on the end of the bed, listening to it all. His face once full of woe now lit up with laughter. 'Norah,' he said, 'you could charm your way out of anything!' The pair kissed and that was that. Things went back to normal and happiness had gained a foothold in the house. No-one was more pleased about that than Lance.

One morning, the nine-year-old came to Norah's room as she was taking her breakfast. 'Mummy, mummy, are you really going to marry Uncle Bernard?'

'Where have you heard that darling?' Norah quizzed the excited boy.

'Mummy, everyone knows. All the servants are saying you are going to be Lady Docker. And you can't be that without marrying Uncle Bernard, can you?'

'Well darling, yes, you are right there. Would you like me to marry Uncle Bernard?'

'Oh yes, mummy,' Lance whooped. 'Shall I go and tell him now?'

'It's only eight o'clock, darling. Let's wait a while.'

That afternoon Bernard planned a drive to the country and a picnic for the threesome. While driving down the lanes, taking in the scenery, Lance could contain himself no longer. 'Do you want to marry mummy, Uncle Bernard?'

'Do you think that's a good idea?' Bernard asked.

'Oh yes, I think it would be wonderful .'

Lance had popped the question on his mother's behalf. And days later Bernard acted on that at a shooting party.

Norah watched in pride as Bernard showed Lance how to shoot, the pair continuing to build a close relationship. She had only one problem. She didn't love the chap. She would use the word 'love' without really feeling it, cared for him but was not head over heels. Norah says she made no secret of this and so could not be accused of leading him on. She felt that love would progress as married life progressed.

Another issue was Bernard's first wife, Jeanne Stuart. Although the marriage had lasted only three months, Norah was worried that Bernard would feel he was making a similar mistake. But Bernard reassured her that if he didn't also feel love would grow he would not enter into a second union.

Norah was desperate for security. In possession of a large fortune and all that entailed she may have been, but that did not provide the social status and security of a marriage. She knew she had to marry above her own wealth and had known few suitors who met the criteria. She and Bernard would be companions, a minor aspect of the bigger picture.

Norah would state frankly that she could never marry anyone poor, not even for true love. Some may find such an uncompromising attitude heartless. But here was someone who, as a girl, knew all about poverty and heartache. Harsh experience had taught her that money and its trappings, along with being fun, also spelled security.

And so it was that on a bitterly cold February day she entered Caxton Hall again, venue for two previous weddings. The Registrar looked on in amusement. Here she was again with yet another millionaire standing next to her. He must have wondered: 'How does this woman do it?'

Before a handful of guests and two witnesses, Norah said her vows again – third time lucky – became Lady Docker, a name soon destined to be on everyone's lips.

The press would be fascinated by these newlyweds' lives as they became more and more notorious. The public would be intoxicated which, in turn, sold more and more papers. They would bring a smile to the masses struggling to come to terms with the aftermath of the Second World War, so loud and vulgar that they took to them instantly.

Lord and Lady Docker were destined to be reviled in high society but effected not to care. That was the old world. By openly consorting with the hoi polloi, they would smash class barriers that had been rock solid for hundreds of years.

They were set to embark on the rollercoaster of fame.

11

•

Lights, Camera, Action!

WORLD WAR TWO HAD IMPACTED on every aspect of society. Britain, like the rest of Europe, had paid an enormous price for its victory. Infrastructure was devastated by the Luftwaffe and the Docker family's steelworks in Sheffield and munitions plants of Birmingham had been prime targets.

Thousands lost their lives nationwide as bombs rained from the skies. The blitz brought London to its knees and, across the land, homes lay in ruins. Children evacuated to the safety of the countryside were reunited with their parents as the public struggled with rationing and the grind of daily survival. Then there was suffering brought about by the loss of loved ones, friends, colleagues and neighbours. Physically and psychologically, the country was in ruins.

It was against this backdrop that, in 1945, Britain voted to elect Clement Attlee as its new Prime Minister. Churchill had 'won the war', the nation decided it was Labour's job to win the peace. As we have seen, Attlee told them what they wanted to hear. He spoke of full employment and, with his cabinet minister Aneurin Bevan, created the National Health Service, the largest social reform act of the post-war period. He also championed nationalisation of public utilities and major industry, horrifying private industrialists. Sir Bernard Docker feared his B.S.A. empire would fall into state hands and be broken up. By 1949, the nation was on its knees and slowly being rebuilt as this fabulously wealthy tycoon and his brassy second wife were thrust centre-stage.

Norah had worked tirelessly with her mercy dashes to bombed-out cities and could even claim to have had a narrow escape herself. For had she not been married when war broke out to Clement Callingham, she might well have still been working at the Café de Paris. Norah, like everyone else in London, had considered the place secure from air attacks as it was effectively twenty feet below ground. 'The safest and gayest place in town,' boasted its management.

On that fateful March night in 1941, the band struck up and the dance floor was duly crowded with couples dancing to 'Oh Johnny, Oh Johnny, Oh!', a big hit for America's close harmony singing trio, the Andrews Sisters. The Café's band leader was the West Indies-born Ken 'Snakehips' Johnson, a major figure on the black British music scene known for his gyrating movements. The performance had only just begun when the first bomb exploded directly in front of the band, blowing poor Ken's head clean off his shoulders. Chandeliers crashed to the floor as a second bomb landed. In seconds, opulence had turned to carnage with over thirty dancers, musicians, staff and revellers killed in the devastation.

Air-raid and ambulance crews helped hundreds out of the rubble. Many survivors were badly injured or maimed. Later, there were reports that looters were spotted picking over jewellery, watches and cash from the dead. Norah got her news the following day from a shocked and grief-stricken girlfriend who had been there. Other friends had not been so lucky and Norah called their families to offer condolences. Not only was it a case of 'There but for the grace of God go I', she knew she was a rarity – one of the few who actually did find the man who would take her away from all that.

That same evening a landmark more iconic than the Café de Paris fell victim to Luftwaffe raids. Buckingham Palace was hit sixteen times during the Second World War and on this particular night a police guard lost his life as the Nazis sought to destroy King George VI and Queen Elizabeth (later Queen Mother) in order to undermine national morale. It was after the first such strafing that the Queen famously said: 'Now I can look the East End in the face,' in reference to her spirit-raising visits to a part of the capital that bore the brunt of the bombardment, trips that doubtless influenced Norah's own war effort.

In short, everyone in the country suffered through that barbaric war and now just wanted – or needed – a little fun, laughter and frivolity in their lives, which is exactly what the Dockers provided.

Formerly, Sir Bernard had been no stranger to stories in the newspapers, primarily regarding his business activities with B.S.A. However, unless you took the *Financial Times* he was most likely seldom on your radar. The general public would have known that he was incredibly wealthy but, really, just another city tycoon until, that is, he slipped a wedding ring onto the finger of Lady Norah Collins.

Norah, too, had been in the papers prior to her third wedding, though just the odd local newspaper piece really, and a few pictures in gossipy society magazine *Tatler*. Now, Fleet Street got the whiff of a sensational story.

The Dazzling Lady Docker

Thrice-married brassy blonde weds Millionaire Hubby Number Three – the headlines wrote themselves. Who was this firecracker? It was manna from heaven and reporters were despatched pronto. And what they found was a media natural who could be replied upon for a good quote.

'What do you think of Mr. Attlee, Norah?'

'Bring back Churchill, I say.'

The press bestowed her with nicknames ... 'Morning Lady'... 'The Lady Who Only Weds Millionaires' ... 'Naughty Norah' and the like. Sir Bernard's fortune was estimated in the early 1950s at some fifteen million pounds, approximately three billion pounds in today's money. Norah now had access to a huge fortune and made no attempt to hide the fact.

'What are you going to do with such wealth, Norah?'

'I am going to spend it!'

Gifts from Sir Bernard were endless. He would lavish a £12,000 mink coat on her for Christmas, buy her sables too, the ultimate in luxury. And what jewellery! The new Lady Docker was showered in diamond earrings, necklaces and brooches; there was even a tiara. She was soon on first-name terms with the movers and shakers of Cartier, Van Cleef & Arpels, and Harry Winston, who donated the Hope Diamond to America's Smithsonian Institution in 1958.

Her dream of becoming like Woolworth heiress Barbara Hutton had turned into reality and every expensive purchase brought more publicity. Before long, she was famous merely for being famous. Rare was the newspaper without Norah in it and with good reason. One editor suffering plummeting circulation put Lady Docker on the front page every day and the decline was halted. In fact, sales began to rocket.

For many, the extent of this fascination was a mystery, but readers fell on every morsel of the couple's extravagant lifestyle. Maybe that was due to how, along with fabulous wealth, Lady Docker had the common touch. In public, she spoke to everyone the same, dukes or dustbinmen. She never hid her humble roots or played the grand lady so the masses could relate to her. The Dockers shied away from traditional high society too, because they were not accepted by the old families of power and wealth who branded them common and vulgar. Once, that would have bothered Norah, now she couldn't care less what a load of boring old toffs thought. She made a show of eating fish and chips from a newspaper in the back of her Rolls Royce – and whatever Norah did, Bernard followed. He became her consort, sitting back and watching while Norah chattered away to all and sundry.

Sir Bernard loved to observe his wife in action and soon realised all this publicity could be used to B.S.A.'s advantage. This 'people's princess' generated acres of press coverage so why not put her on the Board and attract publicity for the company, which could also then pick up the spending tabs! After all, that was how the company had always worked – amalgamating lines to cut costs and create more profit. Little did he know how that tactic would turn out here.

Norah loved shopping. She was like a child in a luxury sweet shop, heaven to her was the world of Chanel, Dior, Schiaparelli to name but three. She was like a modern day lottery or pools winner – spend, spend, spend. And she did, did, did, determined to damn well enjoy it. And given how she liked to spread her cash around, shopkeepers were Norah's best friends. Not surprisingly, they adored it when a gleaming Docker Rolls pulled up outside and, as an added bonus, they were mentioned in the newspapers the next day, bringing more customers flocking to their store in the hope of meeting Naughty Norah in person.

The interest in Lady Docker even ran to a headline and photograph in one paper showing her buying lampshades in the Sloane Square department store Peter Jones. Staff would fight to attend to Norah because she was such a big customer and a character, unlike some other ladies who would agonise over a reel of cotton.

She was chatting one day to a salesgirl about the latest fashions and the girl said: 'Have you seen our new swimming costumes, Lady Docker?'

'No, I haven't,' Norah replied.

'Esther Williams has bought one just like this,' the girl said breathlessly, of the famous swimming movie star.

'Well, if it is good enough for Esther Williams, it's good enough for Norah Docker,' she said. 'I will take it in six different colours – and pick one yourself as well, dear.'

The girl thanked Lady Docker profusely, telling her she was very kind.

'Not at all,' she said. 'Call me Norah, and I will see you next week. Oh, and keep reading the movie magazines, I like your tips!' And with a swish of mink coat she was off to spend more money.

Who better, with a little coercion of board members, to become the new public ambassador for B.S.A.?

12

•

Show House and Show Cars

ONCE NORAH WAS ON THE B.S.A. board, the astonishing amount she spent could be put through the company as legitimate promotional expenses. This bright idea would ultimately bring the Dockers crashing down but, at the time, everyone thought it genius.

One Norah quip made the front pages. When a reporter asked for her favourite food, she replied: 'Bangers and mash.'

Result: mirth across the country.

Such publicity, though, was completely at odds with how the Dockers really lived. While many everyday Brits did begin to enjoy rising disposable income as the economy grew in strength and confidence, Britain's most popular celebrity pair were awash in houses, yachts, cars, jewellery and all the publicity that came with them, hardly the same existence though chiming with the surge in optimism and ambition.

Norah could create more interest in a day than a battery

of B.S.A. publicists or Hollywood agents could muster up in weeks. She loved to throw lavish parties, almost always at her home from home, Claridge's, next door.

One of her most famous parties made every front page heralded as the 'party of the century' by the press. It was a gathering of the cream of the jetset and cost many thousands of pounds, drawing guests like British showbusiness figures Jimmy Edwards, Gilbert Harding and Lady Isobel Barnett, and Hollywood sex bomb Jane Russell, all of whom would form unlikely friendships with the Dockers for many years.

It was now that the first newspaper dubbed them 'the Dazzling Dockers,' with readers given details of the goings-on ... food and drink served on silver platters by footmen in full livery ... dozens of orchids flown in from France and Spain. 'No bangers and mash tonight,' they wrote. In the wee small hours, bacon rolls were served and goody bags handed out with Steiff soft toys inside. The paparazzi did their thing and people began asking for her autograph on the streets. She loved all of that, of course, surrounded by adoring fans.

All those years ago she had dreamed like many young girls of being a Hollywood star. Well, this was a level of stardom on a par with that, with the added bonus that family business B.S.A. was also basking in the blaze of publicity.

At another party the Dockers bid against one another to raise cash for a favoured charity. They autographed menu cards and sold them for between 2/6 and £5 each. This gave the papers more celebrity controversy when a disgruntled Gracie Fields 'stomped out of the ballroom'. In many ways, Norah had stepped into the shoes of 'Our Gracie'. The much-loved northern comedian, alleged singer and cinema box office money-making machine had been hugely popular, the 'Forces' sweetheart' no less, but was also accused of fleeing to the USA when Italy entered World War II. In fact, she had little choice. Married to an Italian, film director Monty Banks, it was either freedom in exile or incarceration at home, but the press – then as now – liked to keep these things simple, preferring to stir the fuss up. Gracie was even criticised in parliament, though apologised to later once the facts became apparent. The fact that she toured the world entertaining the troops was also overlooked in some quarters, but there is no doubt that her popularity would never again reach its pre-War height. Norah, on the other hand, had gallantly chosen to stay in England and see the war years at first hand, hadn't she? She was the working class girl made good now, not Gracie Fields. The press reported that the Dockers earned hundreds of pounds that evening and matched it pound for pound from their own pockets. Gracie Fields, they wrote, had contributed nothing.

Norah was photographed everywhere, from parties to premieres to charity marbles matches. Norah was an avid – and very competitive – marbles player, as we have seen she'd get her chauffeur to stop the car so she could join children for a game in the street. At one gala evening, she had her picture taken with Princess Marina of Greece and Denmark who was also the Duchess of Kent, the King's sister-in-law. She could not take her eyes off Norah and her stunning £2,000 silver and mother of pearl embroidered Dior gown finished off with a blaze of diamonds and tiara. Alongside that, the widow of the Duke of Kent looked homely. But the biggest satisfaction was that Princess Marina now knew who she was.

After complimenting her on the gown and bling (which she said was 'almost regal') the princess invited the Dockers to watch the gala from the Royal Box. Little old Norah Turner from Derby hobnobbing with the European elite, toast of the town and Fleet Street's front page girl. Sometimes she would think: 'Is this really me they are making all this fuss about?'

The Dazzling Lady Docker

Norah could also now fully indulge her passion for fashion. From being very young she had spent large amounts on her wardrobe. Extremely rich and famous she could shop with British couturiers Norman Hartnell and Hardy Amies, the latter having designed the young princess Elizabeth's wedding dress for her marriage to Prince Philip, the Duke of Edinburgh, on 20 November 1947 at Westminster Abbey.

Norah had also her own dressmaker, Fanny Chiberta, who over the years would make her hundreds of outfits. All Fanny's gowns were of the finest lace and tulle, embroidered by hand with thousands of beads and rhinestones. She would drop any other client to please Lady Docker.

'You're better than Dior, Fanny darling,' Norah would gush, upon spending another thousand pounds.

The staggering bills were passed on to Sir Bernard, who was pleased that the press called her the best dressed woman in the country. He spared no expense, paying for perfumes from Chanel, ocelot furs, crocodile handbags and shoes by Miss Peacock, supplied by companies who counted the Queen Mother and Princess Margaret among their stellar clients.

Norah had a personal hairdresser too, Martin Douglas, who was also visited by royalty and the society ladies at his Mayfair salon. Norah had her hair done and set daily by him. No-one else but he was allowed near it. Margaret, Duchess of Argyll allegedly moaned: 'I'm a Duchess, but I still have to wait until Lady Docker is done!'

Hair done, Norah would then have a French manicure and possibly a massage – her morning routine. If she was going to a ball or special event, Martin Douglas would come to the house to prepare her for the evening. Where Norah's previous two husbands could be tight to the point of miserly, according to her calculations, no such accusation could be hurled Sir Bernard's way. If Norah wanted something she got it, whatever the price. Nor, it seems, did the man find it easy to say no to anyone else. Once, in St. Moritz, he paid £50 for round after round of drinks as members of freeloading café society gathered around. Norah felt it her god given right to spend Sir Bernard's coin, yet could be very caustic to those she believed were taking advantage of his good nature.

The Docker publicity machine rolled on, daily articles churning off the presses. For all the occasional brushes with royalty, however, society's higher echelons continued to abhor their behaviour and seldom included the mega-rich couple in invitations to aristocratic gatherings.

'They are not interested in me and I am not interested in their outdated pretentious rubbish,' Norah told a friend at the time. 'They are not going to tell me how to behave with dignity or how to spend my money. They can stuff their coronets! I've seen three balls over a pawnbroker's shop, that's reality. And as for *Burke's Peerage*, give me the *News of the World* anytime.'

Nor would it be long before a new medium, television, came calling, eager to glimpse the Dockers' private lives. That came via *At Home with the Dockers*, a long-forgotten precursor to the reality shows of today, filmed and broadcast live.

Enthralled viewers were shown around a mismatch of period furnishings, Queen Anne to faux Louis XVI, Dresden figures dotted around on tabletops and French fireplaces, flock wallpaper completing the gaudy décor. There was also a look inside Norah's huge boudoir, its closets groaning with hundreds of season-coded dressing choices, and jewellery.

Then Sir Bernard took over, showing the presenter more of the mansion. He introduced us to a maid, Edith, who served the couple a simple TV meal. The camera then cut to Norah chatting and then Sir Bernard again, hastily changing into swimming shorts. To round off the couple's first live TV appearance he was to take a plunge into the indoor pool – the fledgling broadcasting service had seen nothing like it.

***

THE DOCKERS WOULD APPEAR ON television many more times over the years, of course. One such programme was *What's My Line?*, when the panel had to guess that Norah was a world champion marbles player.

As Norah was now on the B.S.A. board, she might be the subject of press releases, one such being an announcement that she would henceforth be designing cars for subsidiary company Daimler. She was given an office and set to work pitching ideas to the design team. Daimler, however, was the weak link in the business empire. Its sales were poor and it lagged behind competitors, almost on the point of closure. Norah in fact came to the rescue and, thereafter, the brand would forever be linked to the 'Dazzling Dockers'.

The company made luxury vehicles for the great and the good, including the Royal family for which it held a Royal Warrant. But Norah realised that this alone could not keep the ailing name afloat. True, when she and Bernard travelled abroad they were frequently stopped by crowds craning to gaze at their elegant vehicles but that didn't bring in the cash. 'The only way to keep Daimler open,' she said, 'is make cars for the masses,' something the firm had never done before.

'Think Ford, Bernard. We should make a family car.'

Sir Bernard realised that Norah was correct. Times were changing, middle class families were emerging as potential customers. With his wife spearheading the publicity drive it could be a winner. So Norah was made a director of another B.S.A. company, Hoopers, who did all the coach-building work for Daimler. Norah was now a key decision-maker in an industry she knew next to nothing about, even though her father, Sidney, had run his own car lot. Yet what she lacked in knowledge she made up for in energy, creative ideas and, of course, publicity, the reason she was brought on board. Norah decided that the way to sell to the mass market was to promote a 'luxurious' vehicle that would be the talk of the motor industry and, for the customer, act as a status symbol.

And so, in a corner of her Mayfair home, she began to work on a show car with Daimler designer-in-chief Osmond Rivers. Its tagline would be: 'You, like Lady Docker, can drive a Daimler.'

To be a hit, the car had to be different. Headlines must be grabbed, taking attention from other companies fighting to win market share in the emerging automotive market. But how do you get a car to stand out from all the rest? A number of ideas were mooted, such as using chrome-plating. But no, chrome was practically impossible to obtain in 1951.

'What about brass' Osmond?' Norah asked.

'Too bulky and it needs constant polishing.'

Then Norah had her eureka moment. She thought back to her Café de Paris days and Bradford mill owner Charles. He'd had a gold-plated Rolls Royce in the 1930s, in which he travelled to his textile mills in West Yorkshire.

'That's it,' cried Norah. 'Gold-plated just like Charlie's.'

But Rivers took a practical view. 'Gold leaf,' he said.

Another idea of Norah's came from a chance joke made aboard the Dockers' yacht, *Shemara*. At a cocktail party, Norah wore a slinky black cocktail dress covered with embroidered golden stars. Harry Barker, Sir Bernard's assistant, quipped: 'Why don't you cover the car in bloody golden stars? Like your frock, Lady D?' So the idea was thrown into the mix, the colour draining from Osmond Rivers's cheeks.

'Lady Docker, is that not a little vulgar?' he asked.

The Dazzling Lady Docker

'Vulgar?! Osmond, it'll be the talk of the motor world.'

'It certainly will, Lady Docker,' he said, visibly shaken. 'I can see it now, shimmering all over the panels.'

But it was his job to bring Norah's idea to life. He knew the thing was a *fait accompli*. If this is what she wanted, who was he to argue? Rivers felt the idea to be crass and in just plain bad taste, but Lady Docker would not take no for an answer and, besides, she was married to the chairman.

The golden Daimler began to take shape in Hoopers' workshops, a process shrouded in secrecy in case word got out. All the fittings ... exhaust ... petrol cap ... wheel hubs ... were fitted with richly-gilted leaf. And those stars! A team of artists worked carefully to embellish every single one from bonnet to doors and boot. The car twinkled from every angle.

Inside, it was as lavish as outside. There was a cocktail cabinet made from the finest Australian camphor wood. The upholstery was golden brocade. Each armrest had a modern radio installed beneath an electrically-controlled sunroof. Nothing had been left to chance – the car was to be presented to the world at the 1951 Earl's Court Motor Show.

Sir Bernard was terrified a Daimler competitor would get wind of their idea and rip it off. Mere hours before the car was due to make its appearance the artist was painting stars on the bodywork. Anyone with the time or inclination would have counted seven thousand, all hand painted. When the cover came off, it was unveiled to a fanfare of gasps. Who had seen anything like it? The Golden Daimler was a sensation.

Princess Margaret was at Earl's Court that year and made a beeline for the stand. Crowds pushed and jostled for a chance to see both the golden car and princess. Sir Bernard proudly showed Princess Margaret around and she appeared fascinated by the solid gold flasks and cocktail shakers.

'Much better than what we take on picnics,' she said.

The Golden Daimler stole the show. Visitors headed straight to it, delighting in such over-the-top exhibitionism. It made global front page news too, of course.

'Vulgar!' screamed some headlines. Others were angry that such a car could be made with a Labour government in power, as though they had anything to do with it. However many papers applauded its originality and workmanship, hailing it as flying the flag of British industry.

The car had cost £8,500 at the time which, today, would be around £200,000. So much for marketing it to the masses.

With the Earl's Court Motor Show over Norah decided to see what reaction she would receive on the streets in the Dazzling Daimler. And so with loyal chauffeur Prattley at the wheel she set off for a spot of shopping in London's West End. People had seen the car in the newspapers but could not believe their eyes when it glided past with resplendent Lady Docker sat in the back, waving. Many stood with jaws open in incredulity – for the working classes austerity still bit deep. Parked up, the car drew crowds like a Hollywood film star and traffic slowed to a standstill.

B.S.A. decided that the Golden Daimler should go on a grand tour across the country and into Europe to boost sales. It went to Paris where Norah was not going to miss the opportunity of a little light shopping. The gowns she wore were made especially for the trip by Fanny Chiberta, each designed to match the car and provide starry-eyed interest.

Picture Post normally ran articles on movie stars, but they put Norah on the cover with her gleaming Daimler. The photos were in colour too, rare in 1951, and they also ran a special supplement inside, selling more copies than previous issues featuring screen sirens Lana Turner, Grace Kelly and Marilyn Monroe. It was estimated that Daimler received over £500,000-worth of publicity for the exercise.

The Dazzling Lady Docker

The European tour was followed by trips to America and Australia, again pulling in huge crowds wherever the Golden Daimler went. No marketing guru could have come up with a media sensation like the vulgar car and brassy blonde. B.S.A. decided that, henceforth, they would build a show car to promote their brand every year. With Norah as their publicity machine, how could they fail? And so the duo set to work again for the Earl's Court Motor Show in 1952.

Osmond Rivers had been forced to eat humble pie – now he would just let Norah do whatever she wanted.

And what she wanted was Blue Clover, a powder blue sports car whose bodywork was dappled with clover leaves. The interior was upholstered in blue lizard skin, as were the steering wheel and seats, Norah again colour-co-ordinated. She was dripping with sapphires and diamonds, hair a sleek and sexy blue rinse, powder blue mink around her shoulders. One tabloid called her: 'The best dressed car salesman in the world.' Daimler number two was also a show-stopper and repeated the trick of boosting a once ailing brand.

The motoring industry's big guns in Detroit began taking notice of this English lady's fancy cars. Upshot being that the American executives decided to play the Dockers and Daimler at their own game. They too would design luxury cars aimed at a less elite market. But the Brits had stolen a march on them and the success was down to Norah. Every year, Daimler's show cars were eagerly anticipated. What would Lady Docker come up with next?

As times and tastes moved forward, the cars became more sophisticated, while never losing their lavish appeal. Publicity was guaranteed, essential to Daimler's revival.

As 1954's Earl's Court Motor Show approached, the world's press held its breath. What would the Daimler stand unveil? Very nearly a disaster, as it happened. A 2.5 litre

Daimler two-seater sports car was sprayed in eye-watering deep green with a scarlet crocodile interior. Prattley, Norah's loyal chauffeur, had a sneak preview and was horrified. 'Please, please Lady Docker, don't show that car,' he said. 'The colours don't match."

Put to her in that way she agreed, but the Earl's Court show was only days away. Norah rang Osmond Rivers. 'We have to change the colour, it is ghastly,' she told him.

'We can't, Lady Docker. There is no time left.'

But Norah told Rivers to have it re-sprayed in a metallic grey blue. That should work. Two days later, as Norah stood in front of the car at Earl's Court, the press and public crowded around for a closer look.

'What's this one called, Lady Docker?' cried a reporter.

In their last-minute haste to get it ready, the car had not been christened. Yet quick as lightning Norah replied: 'It's called Silver Flash.' Next day, Norah and Silver Flash were plastered across every front page. She had done it again.

The 1955 show car would be the Docker Daimler Mark V, popularly known as the 'Golden Zebra.' It was a cream and gold effort with an ivory dashboard cocktail cabinet, vanity case, picnic baskets, ivory fittings and solid gold accessories. All had Norah's initials engraved on them in gold – as did the doors. Finishing it off was a chrome-plated zebra mascot on the bonnet, matched by real zebra skin upholstery inside.

'Why zebra skin?' a bemused onlooker asked.

'Mink is too hot to sit on, darling!, Norah replied.

The quote was another of Norah's most famous and made newspapers across the world. Increasingly, though, as might have been expected, competition increased. Spotting a good thing, luxury show cars were soon rolled out by every leading car company, often bearing a cheaper price tag and with a bikini-clad model draped across the bodywork.

The Dazzling Lady Docker

Not at Daimler. Here was the company that invented the annual show car circus and why have half-naked girls flogging your wares when you had Norah? Between them, the Dockers had turned Daimler into a household name and saved thousands of jobs on production lines.

It had been a calculated and risky move to use Norah as a publicity focus, but for the moment no-one could deny that it had also been a spectacular success, Docker and Daimler linked in the national mind. Norah was Daimler, so the public imagined the Dockers owned Daimler. Sadly they did not and, as we will see, it was that which would come back to haunt the couple.

For now, B.S.A. rubbed their hands with glee at the publicity coup of the decade. None of their products had ever received such publicity and never would again. It was a brief window in time when the right person – Norah – and the right product – Daimler – grabbed the international spotlight.

Many years later when the five show cars had been sold off, Norah would let slip over drinks that she could scrape the gold leaf off the Golden Daimler with her fingernail. And while she was at it, she added that the total cost of the gold leaf and labour was little more than one hundred pounds.

'All that glitters is not gold!' she laughed.

13

•

Strife on the Ocean Wave

SIR BERNARD AND NORAH WERE very proud of their gleaming cars – including the five B.S.A. continued to let them use – but their most cherished possession was always their super yacht *Shemara*.

Today we read of Russian oligarchs and their floating gin palaces worth tens of millions. They are a feature of smart Mediterranean ports, often moored in Monaco, where they compete to be bigger and more luxurious than the next boat.

But before the Iron Curtain crashed down in the 1980s, luxury yachts were rare indeed. *Shemara*, a gleaming pleasure palace ahead of its time, was the envy of the super-rich. An invite from the Dockers to cruise on her was highly coveted.

Shemara had been built for the Docker family by Vosper Thornycroft shipbuilders. Ocean going and 212 feet in length, she had an interior boasting six state rooms, including a huge master suite and several stunning reception cabins. Outside, the decks were finest teak wood manned by a sixteen-man crew in uniform. The interior was the last word in luxury and style, the furniture and fittings adding to the nautical glamour. The Dockers loved to show guests around. Like the Golden Daimler, *Shemara* became part of the legend. The Docker family in 19th century industrial Birmingham had been reticent about their wealth. Trappings of success were kept under wraps. Then Sir Bernard married Norah, mantra: 'If you've got it, flaunt it!'

In 1938, when their yacht was completed, war rumbled across Europe and *Shemara* was requisitioned by the Royal Navy. The opulent interiors were mothballed as hundreds of sailors bunked up in the reception and state rooms. She was returned to the Docker family in 1945.

At which point the prized yacht was returned to Vosper Thornycroft for a complete overhaul. There would be a new member aboard too in Norah. Wherever the Dockers went in the *Shemara*, sensation followed. Once docked in the harbour at Antigua, locals regaled tourists that Lord and Lady Docker sat upon golden thrones and ate off solid gold plates. This was completely fanciful but it all added to the mystique.

Shemara hosted guests from all backgrounds, expected to unexpected ... royalty ... heads of state ... diplomats ... film stars and, most famously, Yorkshire miners. Norah always made a point of inviting local children aboard and entertain them with more games of marbles. They adored this female pied piper and lapped up being on such a yacht of course.

Norah is quoted as saying that *Shemara* brought her more happiness than all the other biblets the super-rich take for granted. Norah's first voyage on her was her honeymoon. She had been spellbound by the grace and opulence, never seen anything like the vessel, one of the few times she was genuinely lost for words.

Shemara was manned by Captain Hector Tourel and his crew, dressed like royal troops with gilt buttons and gold brocades highlighting their immaculate tailoring. Greeting the newlyweds, they presented the happy couple with a huge silver salver engraved with the whole crew's signatures.

Norah was overwhelmed by that. Not even Blenheim Palace had such an effect on her. When Thornycroft had built *Shemara* it had cost the huge sum of £100,000, today that's several million, and of all the Docker's homes was the most expensive to maintain. Day to day running amounted to over £30,000 a year. Kept in tip top condition she was ready to sail at any time. The name *Shemara* is Gaelic, translating as 'peace and quiet at sea.' With Norah at the helm and Sir Bernard her first mate, there would be little of that.

Shemara was the ultimate status symbol. Intoxicating and beautiful, many of Norah's most famous and infamous publicity coups revolved around the craft. Once, in Capri, a rather-the-worse-for-wear Norah and Sir Bernard were being driven back to her after dinner and too much to drink. They were stopped by a ferryman. Taxis were not permitted on the jetty where *Shemara* was moored, leading Norah into a heated argument. The irate Italian began to shout and Norah in her drunken state shouted back: 'In the name of Gracie Fields, I demand justice!', Gracie being Capri's best known resident. Having realised he had not removed his cap in the presence of a lady, she then removed it for him and hurled it onto the ground. What Norah failed to realise, though, was that he was armed with a gun, the sight of which quickly brought her to her senses. So down the quayside she limped, with Sir Bernard hot footing it behind, a trivial incident that caused unpleasant headlines and would come back to haunt them.

For now, she was Lady Docker and the great and good beat a path to her famous door. Sometimes these meetings ended in disaster, or tears, and occasionally real friendships were formed. An uninvited guest to the *Shemara* was Farouk, the former king of Egypt overthrown in a military coup in 1952. He spent the remaining years of his life in enforced exile. The Dockers were moored in Cannes when he arrived and began banging heavily on the window.

'Good god, it's Farouk,' yelled Bernard, aghast.

Norah refused to receive the exiled king and he strode off in a huff. He and she had a lot in common. He also was a spendthrift but put Norah in the shade with his predilections for jewellery, ostentatious homes and sumptuous furnishings. Like Norah he loved the gilded style of Louis XVI furniture but she and he didn't see eye to eye.

Months later, the Dockers did invite Farouk to dine with them and other guests. Norah was a noted hostess and all were plied with the finest foods and wines whatever their social standing or background. But that night everyone looked on in horror as Egypt's former ruler devoured huge amounts of food and then demanded more. Double cream was poured on every course, Norah disgusted at his gluttony. The deposed monarch would never be invited again.

Another guest to be given short thrift was Lord Duncan-Sandys, Conservative Member of Parliament and son-in-law of Winston Churchill. Best remembered today for speculation in the tabloid press that he was the 'headless man' in the scandalous Margaret, Duchess of Argyll divorce case trial of 1963 – wherein, as we have heard, the divorce case centred around photographs of the Duchess fellating a naked man whose face could not be seen – he had offered to resign from the cabinet in the ensuing media frenzy. Invited aboard by Sir Bernard, there was a lot of tension between the Tory and Norah, who did not care for him at all.

Duncan-Sandys, picking up on the vibes, turned to his

hostess and asked: 'You don't like me do you, Lady Docker?'
He was shocked by the candour of her reply.

'No, I don't,' she said.

He got to his feet, left the yacht and never returned.

Yet it was not always trouble at sea. One of Norah's
most valued times was when she entertained those Yorkshire
miners. It was also one of her biggest publicity coups as the
world press and Pathé News were there to share in the fun.
The miners had been invited to a B.S.A. factory to see how
the industry worked and the mining industry's role within
it, supplying coal to the company's huge furnaces. Norah
chaperoned the Yorkshiremen around the extensive factory,
laughing and joking with the group. When it was time for the
miners to leave they asked if she had ever been down a mine.

'No,' she responded, 'but I would love to.'

True to their word, the miners sent an invitation to Lord
and Lady Docker to their colliery just outside Leeds. Crowds
lined the grim streets of back-to-back housing as the Golden
Daimler made its way up them. At the colliery gates, cheers
went up, as though for visiting royalty. Norah changed into
immaculate navy blue overalls and, when she came out, the
miners joked that they didn't want her to spoil her frock. She
donned a safety helmet, carefully so as not to over-ruffle her
immaculately coiffured hair, was handed a pick-axe and
stepped into the lift. She and the miners descended the shaft
and a few minutes later reached the bottom, eight hundred
feet below ground. Norah had taken loyal maid Reed down
with her for moral support, Sir Bernard in the next lift.

They made for an odd sight indeed. For one thing,
Norah refused to take off her high heels! When the lift came
back up to ground level and the doors opened on daylight
the crowds cheered again. Flashbulbs popped and cameras
rolled to show a jubilant Norah and her new mates chatting

away, completely relaxed. She would tell reporters how much she had enjoyed herself and how, only the evening before, the miners had given them a royal reception and a lovely dinner of turkey and all the trimmings. Like the rest of the country they knew that Norah's favourite tipple was pink champagne and it had flowed. Norah danced with the miners and had a good old gossip with their wives. The following day's papers approved heartily of 'Lady Docker down the mines."

Norah always appreciated kindness and hospitality in others and had been truly humbled by that of the miners. She had loved their friendly no frills entertainment and decided to reciprocate. So she planned a party on the *Shemara*.

The yacht was docked at Southampton on the day of the party and the miners brought Norah a huge basket of flowers. She pulled out all the stops. They dined on the finest foods including roast beef, Yorkshire ham, salmon, lobster and roast chicken, sent down in large hampers from the same Fortnum & Mason store that had once been owned by second husband Sir William Collins. As Norah told anyone willing to listen, it had needed to be sold off to pay death duties. The banquet was washed down with whatever drink the miners desired and much champagne (pink, of course), whiskey, gin and Tetley's bitter, included to make everyone feel home from home. The buffet ran the full length on deck and there were no social barriers, conversation flowed. The miners loved Norah and she them. She danced and joked, at one point doing an impromptu sailor's hornpipe while a bemused Sir Bernard looked on, chugging at a huge Havana cigar. Norah changed for her dance into a specially made couture sailor suit and the miners cheered and clapped, some puffing away with Sir Bernard.

Norah had yet again pulled off an astonishing publicity coup. Every newspaper covered the story and Pathé News filmed it all for the nation to see in cinemas everywhere. 'Who lives better than the Dockers?' Answer: 'The miners!'

Nobody could do it like Norah. Many would try but fail to create such a media whirlwind. Norah loved it, but Sir Bernard was a more reluctant celebrity. He would stand back, watching from the fringes, his face a picture of bemusement or horror as the journalists got their copy and snappers their photographs. But awkward though he felt, the print runs and viewing figures said it all. Every time she mentioned Daimler and B.S.A. those readers were potential customers. With that benefit in mind, he readily accepted her celebrity status.

Long before celebrities had PR managers and reality TV stars, IT girls and footballers' wives tipped off the tabloids, Norah merely had to show up and was guaranteed press coverage, all good tongue-in-cheek fun usually. However one incident caused the Dockers acute embarrassment and it also brought Norah's love affair with the media to an end. The backlash from it created unpleasant headlines around the world, revealing Norah as spoilt and out of control. It would affect how the public perceived their outrageously wealthy lifestyle and change the tide of opinion entirely.

***

IT HAPPENED IN ONE OF Norah's favourite places in the world – Monaco, where *Shemara* could often be seen docked or cruising down the French Riviera, with stylish parties and dinners in full swing, glittering in the azure sea.

A year before, the Dockers had attended a charity ball and cabaret in aid of the Red Cross. It had been hosted by Prince Jean-Louis de Faucigny-Lucinge, a fixture of society events there and, more importantly, as a French aristocrat, close to the House of Grimaldi who ruled the principality.

The prince was also president of the Monte Carlo Sporting Club and Casino, a role he relished. The gala began well. The Dockers were enjoying themselves with invited guests, but when it came to the cabaret they were not happy. It was little more than a fashion show for Dior. Other guests too were disgruntled. Why should they pay £15 per ticket – a large amount of money in 1951 – when they could go to Dior and see a fashion parade for nothing? Like Norah, many were regular customers and had already seen the collection at his Paris salon. So, in true Norah style, she marched over to the hapless prince's table and let rip her disappointment.

'The cabaret was awful,' she said. 'Could you not have put something better on than a fashion parade?'

The prince sat impassively, then bellowed: 'Remove your wife, Sir Bernard, now. I demand an apology from her.'

That he duly did, though Norah, in a rage, continued to rant to other guests about how inadequate the cabaret was when there came an even bigger eruption. Sir Bernard was soon being restrained by five men and shouted: 'What the bloody hell are you doing?' Norah pulled him away and back to their guests. 'They thought I was going to punch Prince Louis,' Bernard gasped, the incident bubbling over into the rest of what had been a pleasant evening.

Looking for some light relief, the Dockers walked to the casino to finish the night there. But the doormen stopped them and said the couple were not permitted to enter.

'Why?' demanded Norah. 'Get manager Pierre.'

Pierre just shrugged his shoulders. 'I don't know what is going on,' he said, apparently confused.

That was the signal for Norah to push by him with Sir Bernard following behind. The Dockers hit the tables, where Norah started on a gambling frenzy. She threw down chips like confetti, taking her wrath out on the Roulette wheel and croupier. As the ball kept spinning Norah racked up huge losses, Sir Bernard watching in shock. It just wasn't her night. The evening had been a complete debacle and was about to get worse. Walking towards their table was casino president, Prince Jean-Louis de Faucigny-Lucinge, about to burst with anger. Sir Bernard spoke up before Norah could say anything. 'You owe my wife an apology,' he said.

The Prince said nothing but his henchman, heavily set and on his shoulder, leaned over to Sir Bernard and said: 'If I was you, I would leave here fast.'

Ignoring the threat, the couple went back to the table but Norah's luck had not improved and they prepared to cut their losses. As they stood to leave, a commissionaire barred their way. 'You can't leave here,' he said. Norah's fury grew. She hollered but he would not move, so Norah tried a different tack. 'Good, I will stay. Get me and my husband a bed and we will kip down for the night right here because, believe you me, man, I am not sleeping on the bloody floor.'

She spotted a casino official who she had been on good terms with before, but became more and more agitated about how badly, in her eyes, the couple had been treated. Then she really flipped and began slapping the official's face. 'I will never come here again,' she promised. 'How dare you!'

The poor official burst into tears, bearing the brunt of Norah's outburst. She pushed past more casino staff and stormed – or staggered – out of the building and back to *Shemara*, Sir Bernard trailing behind.

Next morning, the local paper in Monaco ran the story that the Dockers had been banned by the Société des Bains de Mer, controllers of the Casino. Its president, Prince Jean-Louis de Faucigny-Lucinge, was outraged by the Dockers' behaviour. He called it totally unacceptable and said it would not be tolerated in Monaco. Norah tore the thing to pieces.

The Dazzling Lady Docker

Sir Bernard moved his belligerent wife along the coast to Cannes, before the pair returned to England. Norah stayed out of Monaco for a year, fuming, but this was just a dress rehearsal for their next fall-out in the principality.

Unable to resist dipping a toe back in the water, Norah came up with an excuse about needing to visit friends, which is how *Shemara* once again came to be basking in the midday Mediterranean sun. The Dockers weren't in the harbour long before an envoy from the Monte Carlo Casino came onto the jetty and asked Captain Tourel for permission to board. Norah braced herself for trouble. She now understood, up to a point, that her behaviour had been poor but was still ready to fight her corner. The envoy, though, carried a huge bouquet.

'It's wonderful to have you in Monaco, Lady Docker,' he gushed. 'Please do accept our most humble apologies. I assure you that nothing like that will happen again."

The envoy could see that his fawning display was working a treat – Norah looked both relieved and flattered – so then played his trump card.

'Would you and Sir Bernard care to attend a gala dinner tomorrow evening as my guests of honour?' he asked. 'I can assure you, Prince Jean-Louis de Faucigny-Lucinge will not be there. His presidency of the Casino was ended over the little affair with yourselves last year.'

Monaco had missed the couple, he said, and wished to make amends for past mistakes. Naturally, Norah was thrilled. She had won and was back in a place she adored, welcomed with open arms, in fact, and floral tributes. With no ghastly prince around, what could possibly go wrong?

Norah marked the couple's return to Monaco society in a stunning gown by the Spanish fashion house Balenciaga, an outfit set off by a suitably dazzling display of diamonds. The Dockers were greeted warmly by Aristotle Onassis, at that time the largest shareholder in the Monaco Casino group. Prince Rainier had brought the wily Greek shipping tycoon into his business as an attempt to lure more members of the jetset to the principality, Sir Bernard and Norah included.

Onassis stood at the top of the red carpet greeting the guests. The Balenciaga gown was the talk of the gala, red and white like the Monaco flag. 'Welcome home,' he gushed.

Norah felt like a royal herself at such treatment. The casino entrance was bathed in floodlights as on a Hollywood opening night, while a battery of press photographers lined the approach. Flashbulbs bathed Norah in a flickering glow, her name called time after time for a better shot while their target simply lapped up the attention.

Such a spectacular display was, of course, merely a ruse designed to attract Docker cash but the couple, with equal inevitability, lapped it up. Norah's friends had already told her that the casino's profits had slumped lately, but that was an inconvenient truth she opted to ignore. Intent on spending thousands at the Roulette table, she willingly leapt back into her love affair with heady Monaco excess.

In 1956, Bernard and Norah received the most coveted invitation in the world. By marrying Prince Rainier III, Grace Kelly would go from beautiful Hollywood dream girl to real life princess, a fairytale to captivate the world. The cynical truth of the matter, though, was that the principality too was struggling financially, all but bankrupt in fact, and so needed such publicity to turn the cash flow around. With the help of Onassis, Prince Rainier had courted a string of starlets in his quest for a suitable bride. His first choice had been Marilyn Monroe, but upon meeting Grace her sophisticated and cool look won his heart and the couple were soon inseparable.

Their betrothal was dubbed the wedding of the decade, every minute detail became international news. Monte Carlo was draped in flags ahead of the big day, excitement palpable. Heads of state would be in attendance, along with royalty – exiled or otherwise – and the cream of English, European and American society, sprinkled with a little more film star magic. Hedda Hopper and Louella Parsons, the movie industry's two 'gorgons of gossip' were there to spill all the latest beans. Norah was asked if she would act as a similar correspondent for London's *Sunday Graphic*. Could she talk about the run-up to the big day, parties she attended and wedding itself? Could she reveal the best and worst dressed guests? Of course she could! Norah added a journalistic string to her bow.

A week before the event, Norah hosted a dinner aboard *Shemara*. Afterwards, Norah, Sir Bernard and guests walked to the casino for drinks. To keep photographers happy, she played the fruit machines in her evening gown and mink wrap, while the private room the Dockers had booked was prepared. Moments later Captain Tourel arrived with news that they could not have the room after all. The entire club had been taken by Prince Rainier. Norah once again gave the casino officials a loud and public earful, before marching her bewildered party to the nearby Hôtel de Paris.

Back on board *Shemara* in the early hours, she woke her secretary, Eileen Phillips, and dictated a letter to the Prince in which she conveyed her displeasure at being unable to use the room she had booked. A crew member was then sent to deliver the missive by hand to the royal palace.

Next day, the Dockers had an unannounced visit from the British Consul. 'Prince Rainier,' he said, 'is most upset with the letter he received in the middle of last night.'

Norah's indignation rose. 'He's upset? What about me? How do you think I feel about being barred again from that bloody casino? He can go to bloody hell.'

'Please, Lady Docker, this is most unhelpful. Prince

Rainier is not concerned by the contents of the letter, merely the fact that your secretary signed it. He feels you have broken protocol and is insulted by your oversight. Could you ask Sir Bernard to come with me to resolve this unfortunate matter,' the consul concluded calmly.

At the palace, Norah's husband duly offered his wife's sincerest apologies as requested, smoothing over an incident that, only days before the wedding, could have caused major disruption for all concerned. Both men talked about their dislike of the press pack tracking their every move.

The following evening, all seemed back to normal as the Dockers attended a glittering performance of the Royal Ballet. Norah had brought a complete style team for the week of pre-wedding festivities, among them hairdresser Martin Douglas, who coiffured her hair twice daily. For the ballet, he carefully arranged it to hold a spectacular diamond tiara in place. Her Dior gown was turquoise and embroidered with diamonds, pearls and turquoise jewels.

His Highness the Aga Khan seems to have been very taken with Norah that evening, whispering in her ear: 'You look stunning,' according to Norah's account. Newspapers too gave Norah's gown most attention. Further trouble was, however, brewing.

On the wedding morning, the Dockers were asked not to drive the Golden Daimler to the cathedral. It had been brought overland especially and Norah, dressed to the hilt in her finery, refused point blank to get on a bus with all the other guests. A flustered Sir Bernard had to calm his irate wife down and find another form of transport, bribing a local taxi driver at a great cost in the end, who risked losing his licence.

As they took their seats, Norah looked around a venue crammed with flowers and the rich and powerful. Along with the Aga Khan, Aristotle Onassis and old sparring partner the ex-King Farouk of Egypt, were Winston Churchill and his son Randolph and the Duchess of Westminster. Writer Somerset Maugham was there, as were movie stars Ava Gardner, David Niven and silent screen legend Gloria – 'I am big. It's the pictures that got small...' – Swanson, to name but three. In fact, the cathedral was a sea of movie cameras, relaying the scene for both film and television. Grace Kelly had given Metro-Goldwyn-Mayer world rights in exchange for a release from her MGM contract.

The bridal gown was a gift from the studio created by Helen Rose, head of the costume department, using the finest lace and silk tulle. It and Kelly's breathtaking beauty drew gasps from the glamorous congregation, although the couple were officially married the day before in the Throne Room of the Royal Palace, an hour-long civil ceremony. As Princess Grace de Monaco the following day, she helped her nervous new groom with the rings as he fumbled around. More than thirty million people around the world tuned in.

Fairytales come in many forms, yet they sometimes do not go according to plan.

London's *Sunday Graphic* had printed Norah's articles and syndicated them to the *New York Herald Tribune*, in which she criticised Grace's fashion sense. She spoke frankly and not a little hypocritically about the blatant commercialisation of the wedding and how distasteful she found it. Heady with the power of the pen, no doubt, Norah wrote that while the world's media heralded the princess a style icon, she did not.

What was she playing at? Norah appeared hell bent on upsetting the newlyweds, Monaco's royal family and most of the residents of the principality.

In hindsight, it's clear she and they were on a collision course. Her outspoken opinions earned her few supporters among an elite who had welcomed Princess Grace into their circle as a breath of fresh air. But the Dockers were huge rollers at the gaming tables, often losing thousands in a single night. And that money was in Monaco. With that in mind, Prince Rainier turned the other cheek to Norah's outspoken rants – a course of action no-one else seemed keen to follow.

In 1958, the royal couple announced the birth of their first child and heir to the throne, Prince Albert. The Dockers, no doubt due to their profligacy in the casino, were invited to his christening. Norah was thrilled. In her mind she put her earlier articles down to friendly advice and turned her thoughts to the next big occasion.

Norah firmly believed that she and Sir Bernard were close friends with the prince and princess. They always gave generously to family and friends but for an event such as this Norah spared no expense. Princess Grace's wedding gift had been an eighteen-carat gold Van Cleef & Arpels compact, with delicate shamrocks as a nod to Kelly's Irish ancestry. They bought Prince Albert a gold cigarette case from the same jewellers, the royal cypher picked out in rose cut diamonds.

At Christmas and Easter, the royal couple reciprocated with signed photographs of themselves framed in sterling silver bearing the Royal Coat of Arms. Norah dotted these around her homes and on board *Shemara*, a none-too-subtle boast that she was the toast of café society. That the friendship was based only on the amounts of cash they threw across the casino table was an idea Norah would not countenance. She would not hear a bad word said about the pair – unless it was from her. If some brave friend tentatively tried to suggest otherwise, she would scream about jealously and wail that people were always trying to put her down.

It was under such delusion that the Dockers arrived in Monaco with their son, Lance, in tow. The card was made out specifically to Sir Bernard and Lady Docker, but this was to be no problem to Norah. She would get Sir Bernard to ring the chamberlain at the Royal Palace and ask for the invite to be extended to include the boy. What could be easier? After all, they were such close friends, weren't they?

'Sorry, it is not possible,' the chamberlain replied. 'We have had thousands of requests and the invites have all been allocated.'

It will surprise no-one to read that Norah was livid at the snub and, in a fit of pique, hoping Prince Rainier would capitulate, she issued a statement announcing that she would not attend the christening. Furthermore, Sir Bernard would not be going either. Having had her say, Norah waited for the all-important third invite. The silence was deafening.

Norah had overplayed her hand yet again, all her past indiscretions in Monaco flooding back to haunt her.

The following evening, the Docker trio went to dinner at the Casino night club. Norah had been drinking all day to drown her sorrows and become rather the worse for wear, although both Sir Bernard and Lance had seen her like this many times before. At their table, she told the waiters and fellow diners how badly she and her family had been treated by Prince Rainier. As the evening progressed, she became more outspoken. Her vitriol and profanities knew no bounds, making for some colourful if uncomfortable entertainment.

Norah had pretty much cleared the restaurant when she jumped on stage and took control of the microphone. She began to insult the royal couple and Monaco itself, calling it a tin-pot principality. Insult followed insult, as her husband and son sat frozen to their seats. Prince Rainier's previous girlfriend, French actress Gisèle Pascal, had been dumped, she slurred: '...because she had no money! Her parents sold cabbages in Cannes market. He went for the Irish navvy's daughter who, luckily for him, was a movie star with a millionaire father. And that bloody lot look down on me! By which point Sir Bernard had heard enough and pulled his drunken wife off the stage.

'Come along Norah,' he fumed. 'You've gone too far this time.'

Luckily the restaurant was almost empty, so not many heard her rantings. Having sobered up the next day, though, she was still furious – seconds out, round two! She and Bernard lunched at the Hôtel de Paris and again the ranting and accusations against the royals began when she started to drink. Bernard was fed up and Lance acutely embarrassed.

'I want to go home,' Norah howled, while her long-suffering husband rolled his eyes towards the gilded ceiling.

In the corner of the table was a flower arrangement featuring the Monégasque flag. Full of rage, Norah tore it up. 'We shan't be needing this,' she said. 'Let us go where we are welcome.' They never set foot in the principality again.

For now, the Dockers again headed for Cannes and checked into the Hôtel Barrière Le Majestic. Norah and Sir Bernard had no idea what they'd left behind until a reporter stopped them in the foyer. 'Lady Docker, would you care to comment on your ban from Monaco?'

Norah acted stunned. 'Banned for what?'

'Tearing up the Monégasque flag is an insult to Monaco and the royal family.'

'I did not tear it up,' Norah retorted. 'I was unhappy at how I had been rebuffed over Prince Albert's christening.'

She pushed past the reporter but there was no escaping the unpleasant news coverage that the Dockers were about to receive. Newspapers the world over put them on page one: 'Lady Docker banned from Monaco!' 'Shame on you, Lady Docker.' 'Who do you think you are, Lady Docker?'

Prince Rainier was not a man to be crossed or insulted.

The Dazzling Lady Docker

He had heard all about Norah's drunken outbursts and how she had dared to savage his reputation in public – in his own country! Enough was enough and, what's more, given an alliance treaty with France, the Dockers were not only banned from Monaco but the entire French Riviera.

Norah had single-handedly created a public relations disaster, both local and international. If you had not heard of Lady Docker before the Monaco affair you most certainly had now. Her reputation, or what was left of it, was in shreds.

The one-time darling of the tabloids was reviled as spoilt, bad-tempered, rude and vulgar, turned on with full venom. In Monaco, the Minister of State issued a statement. 'The Prince's government,' he sad, 'has been obliged to take administrative measures of the expulsion from its territory concerning Lady Docker, who indulged in public demonstrations offensive to the Prince and his principality.' More such statements followed, publicly denouncing Norah.

Sir Bernard knew Norah had pushed her luck and that this was a diplomatic blunder of epic proportions. Hundreds of reporters and photographers descended on the Majestic, eager to get a photo of the most hated woman in Europe.

'What are you going to do now, Lady Docker?' they heckled, hoping to catch a negative reaction as the flashbulbs popped in their target's face.

The press pack camped out in front of the hotel, the Dockers now under siege inside its elegant portals. Two days later, two government officials delivered the formal expulsion order and again the Dockers were front page news. Next day, Christening gifts sent to baby Prince Albert were returned to the couple's suite, including a Cartier gold watch.

Needless to say, all of this hit Norah hard. The family made their escape to England, Cannes, too, happy to see the back of them. The Dockers now feared a backlash at home and had every reason to do so. Huge crowds descended on London Airport as the trio trooped off their aeroplane in shame. The press pushed and shoved and one reporter thrust out a Monaco flag: 'Care to tear up another, Lady Docker?'

'No, thank you,' she snapped back.

In the airport lounge, a flustered Norah gave a press conference in which she attempted to calm the sorry episode down, answering reporters' questions in a curt but matter of fact manner. It was obvious the situation had got to her. The woman who had once laughed and joked with the media was now a rabbit caught in headlights.

Yet more reporters were outside their Mayfair home. The Dockers were a *cause célèbre*. Sir Bernard took the matter in hand and instructed a solicitor to reach some sort of a compromise with Prince Rainier. After a number of attempts the man was finally granted an audience, at which he was told that the couple would be welcomed back to Monaco – if Lady Docker made a full public apology for her behaviour and all the opinions she had aired about the royal family.

Of course, Norah refused. After everything, she still felt it was the Prince who should telephone her to resolve the affair. It was she who was owed an apology and explanation. And if he, Prince Rainier, didn't produce it to her satisfaction, she would take him and his government to court.

Sir Bernard, however, put his foot down on that one, telling her a 'fight for justice' would only raise the hostility and open them up to more ridicule, from which only lawyers and the press would benefit. One tabloid went so far as to report that Norah wished baby Prince Albert dead. She was in tears at such malice and wrote to Princess Grace telling her of her love for children and that she would never say such a thing. Weeks later, she received a reply: 'Lady Docker, I have learned to ignore such rumours and appreciate your writing.'

The Dazzling Lady Docker

Many mocked the Dockers heartily. It was the general opinion that they were architects of their own downfall. But there was some support in the *Daily Mirror*'s 'Cassandra' column: 'I was surprised and amused at the tetchiness of the bristling little Prince and his bride from Walt Disney land. But really what was astonishing was the monumental block-headedness of the French who spend millions of francs trying to get foreigners to go to the French Riviera,' declared the paper's humourous writer, William Connor. 'The Dockers, with their mighty yacht *Shemara* were the finest possible advertisement for the dizzy playgrounds of Europe. Little Brigitte Bardot was a poor successor! If the Dockers had never been born the French travel industry and publicity boys would have had to make them up.'

Norah loved that article. She sent a copy to Prince Rainier to prove her point, but this time received no reply.

Norah said she was bored anyway. It was full of old ladies and decaying riches. Obviously the remark about old ladies was a dig at Sir Bernard's first wife. Norah told the press she would open her own resort with casinos, hotels, restaurants and the rest just to show them, a lot of hot air.

The truth was, Lady Docker could no longer bear to hear Prince Rainier's name mentioned in her company. She blamed him for all the misery and bad publicity. He was the loser not she. In reality, the volatile chapter was the beginning of the end. Cut adrift from the jetset and café society, the gates to the international playground slammed shut.

14

•

The Pink Panther

WHETHER FAVOURED BY THE JETSET or not, Norah was seldom out of the newspapers throughout the 1950s, meaning that the Dockers' vast wealth and associated lifestyle were of course public knowledge. This led to a couple of robberies that the press dubbed 'Britain's Biggest.' In the first such heist, a huge ten-carat diamond ring that would inspire the comedy film *The Pink Panther* was purloined.

Bounty from three millionaire husbands, her jewellery collection had seen her dubbed 'Mayfair's Richest Woman.' In her view, she'd worked hard for it. Nobody could sell Lady Docker a dud. She had an expert eye and used it, although added: 'When a man gives you a diamond, never say no.'

The 'Pink Panther' was set into a ring, a gift from Sir Bernard and her prize treasure. Its colour was natural. It hadn't been treated, as diamonds can be, and was one of the most valuable in private hands, today worth several million pounds. When Norah wore the ring it caused a sensation, all part of the Docker publicity machine that helped to make them the most talked about couple in the country.

But there were other people interested in the Dockers' possessions. The London underworld, for instance, and in particular the Pink Panther. In December 1954, a party was thrown at Claridge's and the two hundred guests included such high-profile figures as the star of the future film, Peter Sellers, Max Bygraves, Hollywood sex siren Jane Russell, the Woolworth heir Barbara Hutton and her flamboyant cousin and fellow New York City socialite Jimmy Donahue. Finest foods and champagne were served to the tune of some £5,000, while Lady Docker dazzled in diamonds.

Many in the know believe that the masterminds of the robbery that followed were the notorious Kray twins.

Born in Hoxton in 1933, their business interests were almost as extensive as Sir Bernard's though of a more shady focus. They terrorised London's East End and beyond. The Krays' empire was built on robbery, arson, protection rackets, and organised crime on a mammoth scale. Their gang was called the 'firm' and greatly feared, its reputation for extreme violence well earned. If the Krays said 'jump' you jumped, because if you didn't they broke your legs. Like Norah, Ronnie Kray loved the bright lights up west.

That being so, the Krays began to take control of West End businesses too, coming to own their own nightclub. The twins loved to be seen mixing with celebrities and people of high office. Guests at their club who were drawn to the allure of the gangster – Judy Garland, Diana Dors, Frank Sinatra and Lord Boothby, Bob to his friends, popped by. The latter was an enigmatic Tory cabinet minister rumoured to be Ronnie Kray's secret lover. Either way, his patronage afforded the evil duo immunity from the law plus cash, booze, drugs and rent boys. He supplied them with a thin veneer of social acceptance and kept Scotland Yard at arm's length.

Whoever the jewel thief was, he must have thought he had pulled off the easiest job in his criminal career. Norah was very lazy when it came to security. She could be very cavalier, believing such things happened to other people, not to her and Sir Bernard. Nobody would rob the 'People's Princess'. For many years, she handed the care and safety of her priceless collection to her trusted maid, who 'carefully hid it' under the mattress each night, telling Norah that she had slept the sleep of gods on her bed of diamonds. No thief was ever going to look there, they thought. A burglar would head straight to the huge wall safe that was always empty.

Then fashionable Mayfair met with a spree of robberies. The police, assuming a cat burglar or some such, had no idea of the culprit. This Raffles-type character left few if any clues and made off with thousands of pounds' worth of gear. With danger in mind, Norah relieved her maid of responsibility for protecting her hoard and decided to find a new hiding place. Ever the trend-setter, she covered the bidet in her ensuite bathroom in a floral chintz material – when it wasn't being used as nature and Armitage Shanks intended, of course – and made an unorthodox hideaway out of that.

'Who would think to look in a bidet?' she asked. 'Still less a bidet that looks like a stool. It's as safe as the Bank of England.'

Alas, it was not. The Dockers returned home one day and nothing seemed amiss. Norah had left some pearls on her dressing table, intending to take them to Cartier to be restrung, and these were still there. They retired for the night and the following morning, after breakfast, went to retrieve a diamond brooch she was planning to wear for a lunch date with a family member. When she opened the bidet, though, the boxes lay empty, their costly contents gone, including the Pink Panther. The infamous cat burglar had struck here too, a £250,000 haul Britain's largest domestic robbery at that time. For once, Norah was simply lost for words. She managed to telephone Sir Bernard, who rushed to his wife's side. When he arrived, she was calm and collected with no sign of tears. Sir Bernard had expected her to be in meltdown.

The police searched the property looking for clues but as usual found nothing. No fingerprints or anything else to go on. Well, apart from the toilet at the scene of the crime. The officer who quizzed Norah was disbelieving. 'What, you kept thousands of pounds' worth of jewellery in a bidet?'

Another officer asked: 'What is a bidet?' They weren't exactly commonplace back then. Norah would laugh at that later but, for the moment, fought to keep her composure.

The thief or thieves had come for one thing: the Docker diamonds. And it would appear they knew just where to find them. Considering the unusual storage place, the police had one particular suspect in mind – the maid. Only she and her employers knew where the jewels were hidden. To Norah's horror, the police took the hapless girl in for questioning where, under interrogation, she admitted to having left some French doors open. The police were convinced she had been the conduit, but the maid continued to plead innocence.

Norah trusted her implicitly but, as the days dragged on, began to have agonies of doubt. The maid remained their number one suspect, though insisted she would never tell and had never told another living soul about the whereabouts of the jewellery. So the investigators sent a team of officers to her sister's house, where a search of the property – even the garden was dug up – drew a blank.

Norah had a heart-to-heart with Sir Bernard and told him she believed the loyal maid would lay down her life for her. 'I know she is innocent,' Norah said. 'She slept with those jewels for years and nothing went amiss. Yes, she was stupid and careless to leave the French doors open, but I know she had no part in this robbery.'

Sir Bernard listened to his wife's defence. Then, flicking the ash from his Havana cigar into an ashtray, said: 'I never doubted her for one minute,' and back the maid came.

The next ordeal came via the insurance company, who were convinced that the three were in cahoots, making the whole thing up. Norah exploded in fury. Not only had she lost her beloved collection, she was also being accused of fraud, with her husband and maid cited as accomplices.

Adding insult to injury, £50,000-worth of the jewellery was uninsured because Norah had not got around to adding them to her policy. The insurance company was confident it would not have to settle this huge claim, but they reckoned without the person making it. She screamed and shouted at the loss adjustors, but got nowhere so went to the top and continued her rampage at their boss. They kept insisting that there would be no pay out due to their suspicions.

Norah decided to fight fire with fire, threatening legal action and nasty headlines for their business. There was no evidence of any kind to say this was fraud because it was not, as justice would prove. It took months of arguments, but the insurers did finally pay up on the £200,000-worth insured.

When the cheque came, Norah high-tailed it to Cartier and had the lost gems remade from archive drawings. Some like the Pink Panther ring, could not be replaced, but Norah was pleased to have most of her collection back. This time, Sir Bernard had it deposited in a bank vault. If Norah wanted to wear a particular piece either Sir Bernard's secretary or the trusted maid would go to the bank to retrieve the item, taking it back once it had been worn. With Sir Bernard now its custodian, the jewels were safe and Norah soon added to the pile. Yet, just a few years later, another superb collection was again the talk of the newspapers.

Sir Bernard believed a second robbery impossible but he could not be more wrong. From another act of carelessness the Dockers fell prey to the country's second largest jewellery robbery. 'How could this happen twice?' Norah cried, as a new avalanche of publicity swept over them, many revelling in their misfortunes. One again a finger of suspicion pointed towards gangsters, but this time Norah decided the police were little or no help. She would solve this robbery herself and decided on a direct approach to 'King of the Underworld' Billy Hill, to help her recover her missing gems.

This second robbery began when the Dockers had a tiff in 1959 and Norah went to Bournemouth on her own, just to show Sir Bernard who was boss. Seated in a first class rail carriage, she was swathed in minks and carried Louis Vuitton luggage. Not surprisingly, this created a lot of interest in her fellow passengers. Never happy on public transport, she felt a stiff drink would help her through this horrendous ordeal and toddled off to the train bar.

A double gin and tonic would drown her sorrows.

'Let me get that for you,' said a handsome young man.

Norah accepted his offer and they chatted all the way to the south coast where, on arrival, Norah invited her travel companion back to her apartment for a nightcap. He accepted and the two continued to knock them back. She told the stranger about her argument with her husband, how she had never walked out on him since they were married and that she was not in the habit of picking up men on trains. He said they should go for dinner in Poole, called a taxi and went off with her to a restaurant, where she was recognised by all.

'Who is that handsome man with Lady Docker?'

One curious diner bribed a waiter to ask how was Sir Bernard was, at which question Norah flushed bright red. 'He's very well, thank you for asking,' she replied.

In the taxi back, Norah had a sudden fit of guilt and said she was going home to her husband at Stockbridge, the Dockers' country estate. She instructed the driver to take her there, thanking the stranger first for looking after her in her hour of need. 'Come to lunch tomorrow at Claridge's as a thank you,' she offered. And that he did, Norah showing the chap that her and Sir Bernard's bond was strong. There was no place for a third party in their marriage. Norah invited her new friend to a party in Southampton too, where she had been asked by Martin Douglas to open his new salon.

Days later, the Dockers drove to Southampton in their Rolls from Stockbridge. Norah brought her jewellery with her as they planned to travel on to see friends. The gems were in a heavy leather attaché case, combination locked. Sir Bernard covered it with a tartan car blanket and left it out of sight.

Norah cut the ribbon to declare the salon open and soon the party was in full swing. Sir Bernard and the stranger went off to find a place to park the car; the man said he was familiar with Southampton and its narrow back streets. He pointed out a spot where the vehicle would be safe. The pair left it there and rejoined Norah and Martin at a nearby hotel. Everyone was having a fine time, especially Norah. She was loving holding court for her friends and hairdresser.

That merriment, though, was about to be shattered. As the time came to depart, Sir Bernard and his new friend had left to collect the Rolls Royce and got back to the hotel a few minutes later. Sir Bernard walked over to his wife, who was still in full swing. On seeing his face Norah knew something awful had happened. Was it Lance? Ashen-faced, he said: 'Your jewellery has gone.'

167

'No, darling. You must be mistaken.'

Bernard telephoned the police, who came immediately to take details of the theft. Could the Dockers come to the station to give further information? As with the first robbery, the police found it difficult to comprehend how the Dockers could be so reckless as to leave £150,000-worth of jewellery on the back seat of a car – more especially a Rolls Royce!

Something else police were unable to fathom was the mysterious stranger. Norah's convoluted tale of their meeting on the Bournemouth train after her tiff with Sir Bernard did not quite cut the mustard. Again, although they were the victims, suspicion fell on the couple. The police thought there must be more to it than met the eye – the Dockers must have enlisted the fellow to help them set up the crime.

It was 04.00am when the Dockers left Southampton police station, bleary-eyed and in a haze of confusion. The newspapers again had a field day. There was little sympathy on display. The Dockers were scolded for their scant security of such valuable items. One tabloid, dripping in caustic rhetoric, vilified them with the headline: 'Easy come, easy go.'

Scotland Yard again came calling, people telephoned with tip-offs. One caller said the jewels had been spirited away on the *Queen Elizabeth* which set sail from Southampton the day after the robbery. The FBI were contacted but no leads were found. The great mystery was that the Rolls had not been broken into. Who had done this, Houdini? How could jewels be removed from a locked car if it was not an inside job? The police felt the Dockers knew more and the formerly adored pair were widely lambasted for carelessness.

Soon, crank calls were bombarding them daily, offering information for cash. Norah's train friend was under twenty-four hour surveillance. Was he the culprit? Had he recognised Norah on the train and decided she was an easy target?

Cartier supplied Scotland Yard with original drawings of the jewels stolen, which were circulated around the trade at home and abroad. The police even circulated descriptions to well-known villains in the vain hope someone might know of their whereabouts. Again the Krays were discussed only to be dismissed as suspects. It was then that Norah contacted Billy Hill, like the Krays a hardened London gangster with an appetite for publicity and celebrity endorsement.

Early in Billy's career he had mentored the twins. In 1952, he masterminded the Eastcastle Street postal robbery in which a post van containing £250,000 was held up. A bullion heist had netted him thousands. But now his reputation as London's most famous gangland figure was on the wane and his prodigies were taking over.

The odd friendship of Billy Hill and Norah began when their paths crossed at the launch of Billy's book, *Boss of Britain's Underworld*, in 1955. It gave handy tips on slashing someone across the face so as to damage but miss the artery. Norah rubbed shoulders that evening with such luminaries as Jack the Slasher, Larry the Lamb and Big Harry, a quite different crowd to the usual café society elite. Norah found them charming as they made a fuss of famous Lady Docker.

Hill told Norah he was going straight. 'Things ain't what they used to be in my day, Lady D,' he sighed, their meeting caught for posterity. When leaving the launch a tabloid snapped Billy giving Norah a goodnight peck on the cheek. Of course, the photo was on the next day's front pages, just as he had planned and a good many copies of his book were shifted as a result. Like Norah, Billy knew the power of publicity, good or bad!

He added that if Norah ever needed any help or anyone sorting out, to just give him a call – which when her gems were nicked is exactly what she did.

The Dazzling Lady Docker

Sir Bernard, respected industrialist that he was, voiced his displeasure at the connection, but Norah believed if anyone could help find her collection it was Billy Hill. So she gave him a ring and he said, yes, he would be happy to help her trace the stolen jewellery. Scotland Yard too were less than keen, but Billy had been enlisted by Norah and issued a press statement declaring Lady Docker 'is one of us'. He was going to find the thieves and jewellery, he said. The media coverage produced more free publicity for Billy and an even bigger mauling in the headlines for the Dockers.

The press needn't have worried. Even Billy Hill and his web of underworld contacts could find no information as to the treasure's whereabouts. And this time, for Sir Bernard and Norah, the stakes were even higher. The insurance company refused any negotiations to pay out because the gems were not insured in transit. This was a huge blow for the Dockers who firmly believed the jewellery would turn up.

The police believed that the jewels had probably been separated by now and sold piecemeal. The case was quickly closed and the Dockers dazzled a little less brightly when they never came back.

15

•

You're Fired!

SIR BERNARD CONDUCTED BUSINESS DEALINGS and other affairs with decorum and dignity, like the gentleman he was. His marriage to Norah saw him gossiped and written about endlessly, but that was a long way from how he would have preferred to live his life. The world was hungry for any morsel about the Dockers' gilded existence.

As we have seen, the couple did share a belief that all publicity was good publicity. Norah revelled in the attention for the most part, mistaking it for adulation. Her husband was circumspect about his deal with the devil. He would recoil in horror at her more outlandish capers. 'As Sir Bernard looks on...' must have been printed thousands of times.

The media portrayed him as subservient to Norah, under her thumb as she paraded before photographers and reporters, laughing and joking. It was easy copy. He knew it increased the B.S.A. share price, yet hated the intrusion.

The Dazzling Lady Docker

And that was in the good times. When all the positive hoo-hah turned negative and the press began to turn on the pair, the media interest then became intolerable. And, as ever, a public once entranced by Norah's wild antics and frivolity grew bored with her, so ever more controversial stories were whipped up as the widespread fascination waned.

Fame is a double-edged sword. It can give the recipient a real buzz, then become cruel, fickle and unforgiving.

Norah loved the trappings of the super-rich, enjoyed her fame in equal measure. As a child, she dreamed of being a Hollywood star. She used her natural down-to-earth charm and *joie de vivre* to great effect and was genuinely kind to family, friends and charities. Cynics viewed those good deeds as outrageous opportunities for more publicity, an accusation to which Norah's reply would always be the same: 'Fame sought me out, not the other way around.'

Norah's big problem was that once she had tasted fame she could not break its hold on her. It was an addiction. Even as stormclouds loomed and her bad behaviour caused a raft of lurid headlines, she believed in her stardom and the love she felt the public had for her. Like a movie starlet engrossed in studio hype who, when the film flops, becomes a box office nobody. Dust, hatred and bitterness is then all that remains for yesterday's star.

The unravelling and demise of the once dazzling Dockers would be played out for all the world to see, the couple increasingly mocked and ridiculed. Like Louis XVI and Marie Antoinette, the deluded pair didn't see their fall from grace coming until it was too late. They ignored clear warning signs and continued in their rampage of profligate spending until it exploded in a spectacular boardroom bust-up that would have devastating personal consequences.

At B.S.A., concerns had been brewing for several years.

The Dockers had been told by board members and friends to curb their spending and damp down their brash ostentatious lifestyle. Norah told Sir Bernard it was just petty jealously. They needed to live their lives in the glare of the spotlight for the greater good of the company. 'Just ignore such wicked thoughts,' she reassured her doting husband.

Normally, he had a much steadier grip on reality than she did, yet that too was a trait that Norah brought into play. B.S.A. would never wash their hands of such an industrial titan, whose family had founded the entire empire and were one of the majority shareholders. 'Bernard, you are a safe pair of hands. Why would anyone want to get rid of you?'

As time moved on, however, the truth of the situation could not be ignored and colleagues within the firm began manoeuvring to get rid of the Dockers and their scandalous headline-making. Everyone else seems to have understood it was over, but the golden couple were deluded, the chairman of one of the largest conglomerates in the world and one of Europe's most powerful industrialists being urged on to his downfall by his second wife. She would be his and her own undoing, driving them both into decades in obscurity.

In hindsight, Sir Bernard's demise began in January 1953, when he was asked to resign his directorship of the Midland Bank, a post he had held since 1928 and a role his father held before him. The chairman wanted him out, citing the board's belief that the Docker media circus was damaging their high street reputation. Such conduct was incompatible with the bank's moral code, tradition and hard work, so they no longer wished to be associated with Sir Bernard and his vulgar fame-hungry wife.

Sir Bernard believed that his and Norah's lifestyle had no bearing on how he conducted his duty as a board member and refused to step down. The chairman was determined to remove Docker, however, so canvassed the directors to vote to that effect at their AGM to be held in February.

The Midland Bank also sent a letter to shareholders in which it was stated that Sir Bernard was creating unsavoury publicity with which the bank did not wish to be associated. The accused retaliated by reminding them in a letter of his own about his longevity of service. Although his personal life was indeed played out in the media spotlight, he said, this in no way impeded his role as a director of the bank.

He went on to quote three recent court cases in which he had been involved, all settled in his or his wife's favour. He wished to continue until such a time as he could not work anymore. Then came a total *volte-face*. Sir Bernard did resign after all; he was about to be charged with currency offences.

At the time, it was illegal to take more than £25 out of Britain, a law many wealthy people – including the Dockers – disregarded. Embarrassingly, the couple were now charged with contravening it. How could a director of the Midland Bank not fall on his sword over that? Convenient timing for an institution he had served for a quarter of a century. Family and business contemporaries recommended he maintain a low profile and, more crucially, keep Norah out of the papers.

As warning signs go, it was a big one. Yet the couple continued to see B.S.A. as their own private kingdom, the piggy bank or cash cow that paid for most of their outrageous excesses. Sir Bernard's chairmanship was his most lucrative asset, underpinning the Dockers' entire lifestyle.

The Midland Bank debacle ought to have made the pair realise the tide was turning. Had they heeded their friends' advice and stayed out of the papers, things may have been very different. Instead, they thought they were invincible.

The currency case saw the Dockers and crew members of *Shemara* brought to give evidence, sparking another blaze of negative publicity. Questions were asked in the House of Commons where MPs mocked them openly. No-one shouted 'Off with their heads!' but might well have done.

The case cost the couple an eye-watering £25,000 in legal and court costs. Their counsel, Sir Hartley Shawcross, who had been the lead British prosecutor at the Nuremberg War Crimes tribunal, argued in court their infringement of the regulations was trivial, but they lost the case, were found guilty and fined £15. Greater damage had already been done. Had they just pleaded guilty instead of trying to defend the crime, the case would have been over so much more quickly.

With his Midland Bank tenure over, the City then began to wonder how long it would be before Sir Bernard also took the B.S.A. high jump, his crazy wife with him. Questions were raised concerning the Docker's excessive spending and the fact that it was being filed under Norah's expenses. One board member asked: 'What is the company getting for the huge expense incurred in keeping the Dockers?'

Well, huge amounts of publicity, historically, but now it was mainly contemptuous and vitriolic. Media opinion-formers accused the Dockers of thinking they were above the law with a self-indulgent pursuit of pleasure at any cost. One advantage of being chairman of a board is that you can vote for pretty much whatever you wish while you are increasing profits and share prices. But only when they are increasing.

Under Sir Bernard's stewardship, the board pushed every whim and fancy Norah had through, while they were riding the crest of the wave. This too was coming back to haunt the industrialist – how could he have sanctioned such extravagancies in a publicly listed company? Doubts were increasingly raised about his ability to run B.S.A.

One of those extravagances – and a major one – was the purchase of Glandyfi Castle, near Aberystwyth, a beautiful regency Welsh pile bought for £12,500, as sanctioned by the board. The Dockers would entertain in its superb interiors, restored to the tune of a further £25,000. The re-fit included fine French marble fireplaces and rock crystal chandeliers in the principal reception rooms. In a state-of-the-art kitchen inspired by TV cook Fanny Cradock, gourmet meals were dished up for B.S.A. clients from around the world. Bedrooms were fitted with new plumbing and ensuites, but no bidets! Yet Glandyfi Castle was rarely used – a needless expense incurred by a PLC for its chairman and troublesome wife.

Another issue was the cost of Norah's wardrobe, which was also charged to B.S.A. There was the staggering £8,000 paid for a gold and mink creation worn to promote the Golden Daimler in Paris, a 'legitimate business expense'. The Inland Revenue, however, saw it otherwise and refused to countenance such a lavish outlay.

Once the tax inspectors got involved, that was that. The B.S.A. did indeed vote to remove Sir Bernard from his role as chairman of the board. That shocked and saddened him. He could not believe he had been 'stabbed in the back' in such a way. Norah, on the other hand, merely saw red.

For her, the gloves were off. She was not about to see Sir Bernard relieved of his chairmanship without a fight. She entered the fray and gave a husband she had grown to care for very much, a very public show of solidarity.

Once B.S.A. made it known that Sir Bernard had been removal from the board ahead of his imminent stepping down from the top job, a frenzy of speculation erupted in the City, and among media and shareholders. The man himself felt duty bound to issue a statement which read:

'The circumstances which have led to the passing of a certain resolution by the board of Birmingham Small

Arms Company by a narrow majority affecting my position, involve personal disagreements and do not concern the stability of the Company.'

To add to Sir Bernard's pain, a pair of board members he felt would vote in his favour had taken against him in the soon infamous boardroom massacre. One was his cousin, Noel Docker, the other his father's closest friend, Sir Frank Smith. Six directors voted to remove Sir Bernard while three came out in support. Had Noel Docker and Sir Frank voted in his favour he would have remained as chairman of B.S.A.

In his fight for the chairmanship, Sir Bernard sent out 10,000 telegrams to shareholders. He would reveal the facts behind his dismissal, he said, and they could believe in his commitment to B.S.A. Foolishly, Norah believed her pulling power to be much greater than it actually was. While at the centre of the worst publicity the couple had endured, she sent a photograph of herself in a black halter neck and diamonds to the self-same people.

Again she was ridiculed in the press, what else did she expect? She had signed each photo personally and each of the recipients also got a letter which, in a potted version, spoke of her tireless work for the greater good of B.S.A. and all the publicity created by her for Daimler cars. She asked for their help in restoring Sir Bernard to his rightful position, adding that the shareholders ought to have been consulted before her husband was dismissed and insisted she had received no financial benefit whatsoever for all she had done, concluding: 'And I believe I did a very good job.'

Norah did believe it. B.S.A.'s shareholders were more circumspect. Five luxury cars, all custom made by Daimler, a fairytale castle in Wales, thousands spent on couture clothing, not to mention entertaining across the world on *Shemara* or, of course, the *carte blanche* at Claridge's. Who else picked up those bills? None of this could be seen as anything other than financial benefit, however Norah presented it.

The next step, as she saw it, was to convince the world that the Dockers were the injured party, which should restore Sir Bernard to his rightful position. She took out a series of advertisements on television and in the press, full pages telling everyone how committed they were to B.S.A. Everything that had been spent was sanctioned by the company to create publicity for the firm and its products. The TV commercials went out on the newly-established ITV at a cost of £3,000.

Despite his promise, due to legal reasons Sir Bernard could not in fact tell the full story. He could only reiterate to viewers – who must have been rather bemused to see such a thing between adverts for cornflakes and cleaning products – that he had increased company profits. The tens of thousands of pounds the Dockers were now throwing into a publicity campaign to get him back on the board were all to no avail.

Norah now began to suspect a smear campaign against her and Sir Bernard, a deliberate attempt to bring the couple down. Through the B.S.A. sacking, the pages were filled with lurid reminders of Docker excess. Gleefully, it was pointed out that B.S.A. subsidiary Daimler had posted a large loss in the previous financial year. The press blamed Norah for them but she told anyone who would listen she had created over half a million pounds worth of free publicity. But as everyone could see, there had been nothing 'free' about it.

Norah protested that she had never asked for a fee for her services, arguing any film or TV star would command a huge payout for attending the sort of publicity junkets that, it just so happened, Norah adored. The press hit back; not even the biggest Hollywood star of the day, Marilyn Monroe, could command the amount of money spent by Norah.

Another issue for the Dockers was that B.S.A. were on top in terms of public relations. The company was gaining positive headlines while the Dockers were sinking under a morass of mud-slinging they were unable to reverse. And the board had a secret trump card to play that would leave the couple reeling in the dirty war of words.

B.S.A. would claim that all five Daimler show cars had been produced for the Dockers' personal use and not for the purpose of creating publicity for the brand. Daimler claimed, hurtfully to both Norah and Sir Bernard, that the first show car, the Golden Daimler, was so closely linked to the couple and their publicity personas that it was unsellable!

The Dockers vigorously refuted both claims, informing Daimler that they had received a number of offers over the years for the Golden Daimler. But as one journalist asked: 'If the car was made for publicity and not personal use, why was it not sold before the next show car came out the next year?'

The Dockers were under heavy attack on all fronts when an Inland Revenue demand for £20,000 in back taxes on the vehicles was received. Sir Bernard returned it to the Revenue and at first refused to pay up, before taking legal advice that they would sue him for the outstanding amounts and quickly settling it. He also settled another hefty Revenue demand for tax on Norah's wardrobe.

Having done so, Sir Bernard believed it was impossible for B.S.A. to claim that he had shirked his responsibility and, more importantly, the same thing went for the shareholders. However, the tax affair merely fanned the flames of interest in his sacking, so the Dockers called an extraordinary general meeting. Thousands of people purchased just a few shares in B.S.A. in order to attend such an unusual event.

The previous AGM had seen just seven shareholders attend, in May 1956 the Great Room of London's Grosvenor

House was packed to the rafters, standing room only. So many had gathered there to see the very public execution of Sir Bernard and Lady Docker.

Outside, in Park Lane, a battery of press photographers jostled for snaps of the formerly 'Dazzling Dockers', brought down by their detractors. The couple still had support and Sir Bernard held a large stake in the company. He was the largest individual shareholder, but that was not enough. He needed as many votes as he could muster and a massive blow was dealt when one of the largest shareholders in B.S.A., the Prudential Insurance Company, sided with the board.

The strait-laced and old fashioned insurance giant held large shareholdings in many of Britain's blue chip companies and had been shocked by the avalanche of negative publicity surrounding Sir Bernard's sacking. The 'Man from the Pru' owned 218,000 shares, the Dockers between them 120,000.

How could the Prudential support a board of directors that held so few shares? The Prudential investment manager was booed and jeered by Docker supporters in a scene of high theatre. Many in the crowd were baying for blood when new chairman of B.S.A., Jack Sangster, took to the podium and was forced to admit that his shareholding was a mere 2,000.

Norah took to the stage, fighting to keep her husband in a position she believed was his God-given right, a divine right to rule. The cathedral-like room became eerily quiet. What would Lady Docker have to say?

She pleaded with great passion and self-confidence that her husband only ever put the shareholders' interests first. His commitment to B.S.A. should never be doubted and she stressed how, under his chairmanship, profits had risen hugely, enriching the shareholders packed in there today. But Norah's plea cut no ice. A company founded by Sir Bernard's humble paint merchant ancestors in Birmingham and turned by them into an industrial giant no longer had a Docker as its chairman. The Dazzling Dockers had run through tens of thousands of pounds in a futile attempt to keep him in the top job, failure to do so damaged their credibility still further.

Once the darlings of the tabloids, they were now a laughing stock. Norah called it trial by media. The adoring early publicity had now gone sour and it was the B.S.A. affair which finally brought it home to Norah that her publicity machine was broken. She had viewed the press as allies, but treated them with mistrust and suspicion thereafter.

Still, if this was a case of British 'tall poppy syndrome', it had been worsened by the victims themselves. Part of Norah still believed the tide could be reversed but this time it could not. For a while coverage continued, especially when the Dockers bought matching Rolls Royces – number plates ND5 and BD9. It was their way of sticking two fingers up at the B.S.A. board. Norah then accepted an invitation to open a brand new Ford dealership in England's north east, where the press quoted her saying: 'Ford is best.' When one reporter said: 'It's hardly Daimler, Lady Docker,' she replied: 'At least you can get the parts.' For the rest of their lives the Dockers would feel great bitterness towards B.S.A. Norah missed no opportunity to ridicule the company board, its products and achievements, while defending Sir Bernard and herself as the greatest assets the firm ever had.

Over the next two decades the couple watered a once enormous shareholding down to nothing, with proceeds paying for their ongoing high-flying lifestyle and tax bills. Publicity, though, dwindled. Times were changing again and the Dockers were no longer relevant.

Without B.S.A. behind them, they became rudderless, ambling around hot spots with little or no purpose.

And with little or no recognition either.

16

•

Decline and Fall

AS YEARS WENT BY, THE Dockers struggled to maintain a place within the rarefied world of the mega-wealthy.

B.S.A. had paid to maintain *Shemara*, provided the cars and clothes, so the pair began to feel the pinch. Most people faced with a reversal of fortune cut their cloth accordingly, but the Dockers were not 'most people.' For a while, they still commanded headlines, but the feeling toward them changed.

The comedian Frankie Howerd ridiculed Norah on TV, picking women out in the audience and saying: 'Look at her, she's like Lady Docker!' to much hilarity. Despite being the butt of jokes the couple ploughed on with the excess as the headlines grew smaller, along with a once gigantic fortune.

The nasty financial losses began in the mid-1950s; losing the B.S.A. chairmanship had cost Sir Bernard £25,000 in salary alone, without all the perks of the job. Nor did those pesky tax liabilities help.

The second uninsured jewellery robbery, defending the currency violation case and various other smaller court cases left a massive dent in their funds, on top of a still extravagant lifestyle. Norah buried her head in the sand, believing they could never run out of money. Sir Bernard had been one of the richest men in the country when Norah had married him, who would deny his wife nothing. Still, even she must have noticed how since the theft her collection of gems had shrunk.

Her wardrobes still brimmed with fine gowns and furs, the fabled minks, sables, foxes, ocelot and ermine. The couple maintained their country estate and house in London, and of course, there was their floating gin palace, *Shemara*. After May 1956, though, they themselves were forced to pay for all that and it didn't take a financial wizard to predict that such free-spending largesse could not now go on forever.

Without a B.S.A. cash cow, the Dockers soon had to dip into their capital. They began to sell blocks of B.S.A. shares, further diluting their interest in the 'family company'. An idea to bring in cash was to charter *Shemara* out at £3,000 per week. This did not prove lucrative as the yacht was chartered only a few times, costing more in charter fees. Then Norah hit upon the idea that they could open a moored *Shemara* to the paying public, like the English aristocracy did with their stately homes. The great unwashed could be charged to gawp in wonderment at the crumbling vestiges of wealth.

Sir Bernard was less keen and nothing came of the plan. Perhaps the couple realised there was no huge interest in them anymore. During their heady years, they had declined a cash offer for £600,000 for *Shemara*. Declining that offer in typical style Norah had said: 'It's not enough, darling.'

Another problem the couple faced, along with other wealthy people, was the heavy rate of taxation imposed on the very rich. The top rate of tax reached 83 per cent in the pound by the mid-1960s. And for those in the super-rich bracket, like the Dockers, an extra 15 per cent was payable on top of that – an eye-watering 98 per cent. Under the Labour government of Harold Wilson, wealthy people were leaving the country in droves. Among them the Beatles, whose 1966 song, 'Taxman', written by George Harrison, was about that very plight. The Chancellor of the Exchequer, Denis Healey, was unmoved, promising to 'squeeze property speculators until the pips squeak' (not the rich, as is popularly quoted).

Sir Bernard may not have been into buying and selling property, but he and Norah realised that to salvage what was left of their wealth they would have to become tax exiles. And they would have to sell more prized assets, as maintaining their lifestyle on their income stream was no longer an option.

So the couple put *Shemara* on the market with a price tag of £600,000 but this time there were no takers. In such an environment, superyachts weren't top of the shopping list. Had the Dockers been more contrite after their rift with Prince Rainier and eaten just a slice of humble pie they might have been able to moor the thing in Monaco harbour. There they could have ended their days in a place they loved.

But as we saw, it was not in Norah's nature to be either contrite or humble. She would not apologise to Prince Rainer and consequently could never enter his tax exile's paradise. The couple were now reduced to making what many saw as fire sales. When Norah saw Aristotle Onassis one day in the bar of Claridge's, she approached him and came straight to the point. 'Would you like to buy a real yacht?' Sadly, she was rather the worse for wear from drink and went on: 'After all, Mr. Onassis, your *Christina O* is just a converted banana boat.'

Onassis politely declined the deal.

But come spring of 1966, the Dockers needed to sell *Shemara* desperately, advertising her as a presidential yacht,

Norah being convinced she would be bought by a crowned head of state. Yet more disappointment. The eventual buyer of *Shemara* was neither a crown prince nor a head of state. Norah hated him, appalled by business methods that were controversial to say the least. His name was Harry Hyams and his wealth *was* derived from speculating on property.

Norah would rue the day she set eyes on Hyams, who built the controversial Centre Point development in Oxford Street. He kept it empty for years, claiming he could not find a suitable tenant for the huge building. A tough cookie, he had bought and sold for millions of pounds in his career and could always smell desperation in a seller.

Hyams knew the Dockers needed cash and how eager they were to get rid of *Shemara*. He hit the cash-strapped pair with an offer of £290,000 – half the asking price. Sadly for the Dockers there was no-one else interested who could afford it. And so, with great reluctance, they accepted and as far as they were concerned, their beloved *Shemara* was history.

Harry Hyams's reputation preceded him and many warned the Dockers not to get involved with the tycoon. But they had little choice, needing the cash. Days after the sale they were in for another nasty shock. Hyams claimed *Shemara* needed £100,000-worth of urgent repairs, though the Dockers knew the boat was in tip-top condition with an A1 certificate from Lloyds of London so and defended the action.

Hyams took the Dockers to court knowing that the last thing they wanted or needed was an expensive case. He was right about that. But this was a matter of honour and they would defend themselves if it killed them. For once, the High Court found in their favour, stating the only repair needed would cost around £100. Hyams then lost an appeal that caused the couple more stress and sleepless nights and was refused leave to take the matter to the House of Lords.

The affair however had rolled on for some nine months, casting a cash cloud on the ageing couple's retirement fund. Hyams was ordered to pay costs that ran into thousands of pounds. Norah saw his attempt to sue them as a means of knocking £100,000 off the purchase price, but he had not counted on her tenacious nature when it came to litigation.

Unlike the Dockers, Hyams derived little pleasure from *Shemara*. He toured the Med in her, but the yacht remained mostly in moorings in Lowestoft. He occasionally chartered her out and future passengers included a celebrity couple very much on the up, Elizabeth Taylor and Richard Burton, who toyed with the idea of buying her. Robert Maxwell also sailed on her, the newspaper baron who died at sea on his own luxury yacht while his own business empire unravelled.

As Hyams became ever more reclusive, *Shemara* stayed moored in Suffolk for years. Her owner retreated to a palatial country house, Ramsbury Manor in Wiltshire, which he had purchased in 1964 for the huge sum of £650,000. At the time, it was called the most expensive house in Britain. Hyams filled its stunning interiors with one of the finest collections of art and antiques to be amassed in the last century and was often referred to as Britain's very own Howard Hughes.

Norah wasn't impressed. She despised the man for his low-down trick, after having already bought the yacht on the cheap. The Dockers were also sad that *Shemara* was left to deteriorate so badly, soon a rusting hulk of a forgotten past.

But time was moving on and sex scandals dominated 1960s headlines, from the divorce case of the Duke and Duchess of Argyll to the Profumo affair. The latter scandal saw Harold McMillan's government brought to its knees after Secretary of State for War, John Profumo, in his mid-40s, was found to have had an affair with nineteen-year-old Christine Keeler, model and party girl. He had met her for the first time at Cliveden, home of 3rd Viscount William 'Bill' Astor, while watching her skinny-dipping in the pool. More revelations emerged, among them that the young woman had slept with Yevgeny Ivanov, Soviet naval attaché and spy, simultaneously. When Astor and Keeler's friend, the osteopath and part-time socialite Stephen Ward, was then brought into the frame as procurer of Keeler and Mandy Rice-Davies, another model and showgirl, for his rich society associates, he was charged with living off immoral earnings. Every day, new revelations of sexual misdemeanors in high and low places played out before an eager public.

Ward, who the jury found guilty, would go on to take a fatal overdose in a cast list that left the latterday Dockers in the shade. Norah, a former showgirl of sorts herself, was now viewed merely as a figure of yesteryear though, of course, she still believed she deserved attention. Truth was, though, the nation had moved on, a reality to which Norah found it very difficult to reconcile herself. With cash and publicity running out fast, she had no choice but to live a less public lifestyle.

Without B.S.A. and Daimler, the Dockers' lives had become somewhat empty. The company had provided Norah with all the tools and attention she needed to carve a name for herself both in post-War society and perhaps even history. Yet now, the only way she might grab a few column inches was through bad behaviour, slapping a waiter perhaps, or pouring a drink over someone's head while drunk. Even that was fast becoming a regular and thus less-than-newsworthy occurrence. It also make the public dislike her even more.

All of which gave Frankie Howerd and company even more material, contorting his face and pointing at overweight ladies. Eventually, Sir Bernard had enough. He took control of the marriage and told his wayward wife that they were leaving London and selling Stockbridge, their country estate.

They would then escape with what little cash and dignity they had left to Jersey, another place for tax exiles.

The couple settled into a modest bungalow that they christened Côte d'Azur, an ironic reference perhaps to their ban on the Riviera. They clearly still had a sense of humour. But Norah loathed the largest of the Channel Islands. She was bitter that a life lived at full capacity had come to a halt and blamed the Labour government for that – it was their fault that the Dockers had been forced to sell their assets and live on this bloody island, wasn't it?

Before heading for their new home, Norah spoke with Sir Bernard about visiting some old stomping grounds, like the Savoy and Café de Paris. Yet both visits would end in tears and humiliation. In the Savoy ballroom, Norah slipped and the couple were accused of drunkenness. Norah was livid. Yes, she liked a drink, but drunk? Never! The evening at the Café de Paris turned into an even bigger nightmare.

Sir Bernard and Lady Docker sat down to dinner in the gilded splendour of a room where, all those years ago, Norah began her rise. This was the scene of many triumphs, back when she was the toast of the town. But now a very different scene played out. As they began their meal, drunken revellers began to mock the couple. They shouted from the balcony, mimicking camp Frankie Howerd: 'Look at her, like Lady Docker!' Then they began to pelt Norah and her husband with bread rolls, as if trying to win a coconut on a fairground stall. Norah fled in tears, leaving Sir Bernard to chase after his distraught wife.

Norah's happy memories of the Café de Paris had been shattered by a group of yobs. She put a brave face on for their move to Jersey but, deep down, struggled to accept their loss of position and wealth. Sir Bernard seemed to take everything in his stride, perhaps relieved that the circus had moved out of town. Unlike his wife, he was happy to live in more sedate surroundings, but his health now began to fail him.

On Jersey, Norah drank more than ever and would tell complete strangers that their downfall was due to jealously. Everyone had coveted her clothes and jewellery, her money and popularity. She poured blame onto the press and B.S.A. shareholders, and her contempt for Prince Rainier spilled over daily, sneering and scoffing at his name.

But the person she hated most was Harold Wilson, Labour Prime Minister. The air would go blue if anyone dared to mention him. 'Bernard, if it wasn't for that dreadful man we wouldn't have to live in this dump!'

Norah drank to forget, often to be found drowning her sorrows in the Rozel Bay Hotel, below the Dockers' garden. Here she would sit, holding court and ever more lit up while the increasingly frail and feeble Sir Bernard looked on. He'd watch as he always had, leaving her to entertain the throng.

Sir Bernard sat nursing a drink as Norah knocked them back, telling her fellow customers that if she ever set foot in Monaco again she would give that Prince Rainier a piece of her mind. One day, in the bar, a classic film noir played on television, during which one of its viewers turned to Norah and asked: 'Didn't you used to be Lady Docker?'

Norah replied, a little worse for wear: 'I still am, what's left of me.'

Norah's behaviour however was becoming steadily – or *un*steadily – problematic, leading to her being asked one day to leave the pub by its landlord Bert Taylor. He accused her of being worse for wear and inappropriate language, which was offending his customers. Norah was shocked. She had become friends with Bert and his wife, Edna, lending the woman clothes and even a prized mink coat to attend a local gala. Yes, she'd had a few, but was merely high-spirited, as

The Dazzling Lady Docker

she saw it. And so with typical over-reaction Norah issued a solicitor's letter claiming defamation of character.

Well, that was one way to get back in the papers, but it was the Dockers the press focussed on, not poor Bert Taylor. The reports said Norah was out of control. Nor did she make any friends with her comment that the islanders were the most dreadfully boring people who had ever been born.

The halcyon days never seemed so far away ... Lady Docker sweeping into the ballroom, everyone aghast at her gowns and dazzling diamonds, crowned with a tiara. Was this a member of the Royal Family, Americans wondered. Two decades on, she had been banned by a pub in Jersey.

For the reporters she quipped: 'Once, I got banned from Monaco, now look at me!'

As the years rolled by, the libel litigations piled up. She became very vexatious about any insult, real or imagined. In 1974, she found herself in court with a tabloid newspaper. The rag in question had said that Norah was to be banned from another hotel for using naughty words. Norah won the case, but it was a hollow victory. The Rt. Hon. Mr. Justice Melford Stevenson observed of the case: 'The Lady is obviously after banner headlines. A sufficiently large headline would have healed her wounds.' It was a cutting put-down and a telling reason for her motives. Lady Docker received the sum of a ha'penny in damages and no banner headlines.

Having offended the good people of Jersey, the Dockers headed for the sunny climes of Palma in Majorca. Here it seems that they genuinely did seek obscurity and settled into a quieter way of life, caring for one other. But as Sir Bernard fell into even worse health, the couple were forced to leave the Balearics and return to Britain, where Norah placed her husband in a care home in Dorset. It was there, at Branksome Park, that Sir Bernard passed away, aged 81, in 1978.

Norah was a widow for the third time. Aged 72 herself, she felt the loss of her life partner deeply. The man who had done everything for her, who lost a business empire to defend her reckless spending and hunger for publicity, gone. From an unpromising start, Sir Bernard and Norah had grown to share true love and empathy, a happy ending of sorts.

But now Norah was soon consumed by loneliness. They have been such a great team, always there for each other whatever the cause. If Norah was happy, then so was Sir Bernard, yet even at this late stage Lady Docker could not escape unpleasant accusations. She was hurt that in some quarters it was said she dumped Sir Bernard in the nursing home because it suited her needs. Norah just hadn't been in a position to look after her husband, that's all. She had grown frail herself and so there was no alternative. There he could be cared for properly, twenty-four hours a day. Norah had wanted the best for him and could not meet that need.

And now she was on her own. Remarkably, her zest for life remained, though diminished by old age. She still drank a bottle of pink champagne every day, considering it a tonic. She sold most of her remaining jewellery but kept her many furs. She would need them if invited to a glamorous party or premiere. Briefly she returned to Palma, but the isolation was too great and so she returned to England's capital.

London was a city she had cherished and loved since arriving there as a dancer in the 1920s. But of course, the city and its inhabitants had changed like Norah, no longer the richest woman in Mayfair and so forced to spend accordingly. With very little money left, she was faced with the challenge of finding somewhere to live in what had become one of the most expensive cities in the world. As her purse would not stretch to Claridge's, she settled in the slightly less salubrious surroundings of the Great Western Hotel, Paddington.

The Dazzling Lady Docker

The Great Western was a former railway hotel with a handsome façade. Run-down now, it had seen better days, not unlike its once-famous resident Lady Docker. It was there on the morning of 11 December 1983, that a truly remarkable woman was found by a member of the housekeeping staff, having died in her sleep. The news of her death caused no fuss or fanfare. Norah's obituary appeared in newspapers, but in all honesty everyone had forgotten who she was.

Norah had lived her unusual life to the full but now she was gone, a forgotten footnote of post-war Britain. The family told the undertaker to expect over two hundred mourners, ranging from relations and friends to the just plain curious. As it turned out just twenty-nine people attended the service.

Yet let's overlook the tyranny of time.

Very few people have caught the public imagination as Norah did. She was loved and reviled by the press, mimicked and poked fun at by comedians, but for all her chutzpah was as vulnerable as the next person. On a cold December day in 1983, you wouldn't have guessed it at her funeral.

Perhaps Norah would have chosen to go out without a bang? That must be doubtful. She would have loved a battery of press there for her swansong. But for her, the party had ended years before.

At least now she could move on to the next one.

Postscript

•

B.S.A.

After Sir Bernard left B.S.A. the company suffered a steady decline in fortunes. Just like the Dockers, poor management and lack of new products in the car and motorcycle divisions meant the organisation struggled to stay afloat.

A government rescue operation in 1973 led to the takeover of remaining parts by Manganese Bronze Holdings, which still owns the greatly reduced B.S.A. empire.

In 1960, B.S.A. sold Daimler to Sir William Lyons, co-founder with fellow motorcycle enthusiast William Walmsley, of Jaguar motors. He purchased the prized subsidiary for its production line, close in proximity to the Jaguar plant.

As the years progressed and Jaguar grew in popularity, the Daimler brand petered out. The last car to carry the Daimler badge was produced in 2007.

Glandyfi Castle

After the Dockers' fall from grace, Glandfyi Castle was sold as a country residence to Harry and Bettina Lancaster in 1962, and then sold on again in recent years.

The faux Regency Gothic pile – these days an A Grade II listed building – was originally built in 1810 for George Jeffreys, a Shrewsbury lawyer.

More recently it was converted into a luxury hotel and wedding venue, guests enjoying the opulent interiors where the Dockers once entertained. Or perhaps walk a garden path made of upturned gin bottles from the Dockers' tenure.

Shemara

For many years, *Shemara* was moored unloved and forgotten in Lowestoft, Suffolk. Her purchaser, Harry Hyams, had little use for the yacht as he retreated into his reclusive world.

By chance, the co-founder of Carphone Warehouse, Sir Charles Dunstone, saw *Shemara* while browsing through a boating magazine and decided to buy her.

In 2007, *Shemara* was taken from Lowestoft and moved to Portsmouth, ending those years of decay.

Once in Hampshire, she was lovingly restored to her former glory, her reception rooms and state rooms coming alive as they had in the Dazzling Dockers' days.

Today she is back, sailing the world and, as in the 1950s, is the talk of wherever she drops anchor. In fact, *Shemara* has not looked so well since Norah was first mate.

The Docker Daimlers

After Sir Bernard was sacked all the Daimler show cars were sold off with some going as far afield as the U.S.A.

Sometime in the 1980s, Stardust, the 1954 show car, was discovered abandoned in farm buildings in Wales, close to Glandyfi Castle (*see below*).

More recently, it was auctioned by Bonhams, where it fetched £110,000, and has since has been lovingly restored with its 7,000 silver stars and mascot some said was based on Norah's Café de Paris days. It remains a lasting legacy of the golden couple.

In 2006, the Golden Zebra was sold, again in Bonhams, for £177,000. Norah would have been pleased indeed that the show cars survived and are now valuable classic cars.

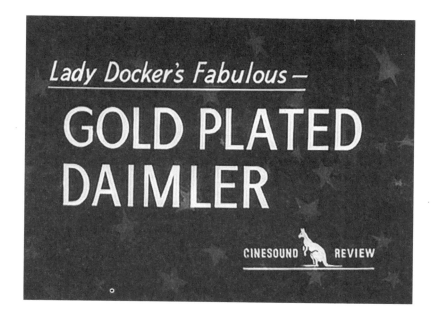

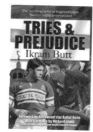

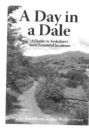

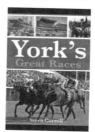

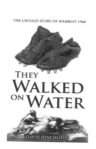

The Barefoot Shepherdess
and Women of the Dales
By Yvette Huddleston & Walter Swan

The Barefoot Shepherdess and Women of the Dales celebrates the variety and versatility of determined women who have made a life for themselves 'far from the madding crowd'.

The Yorkshire Dales attracts tourists aplenty, but most visitors return to their towns and cities, renewed by the peace and quiet of the countryside, though unable to leave their modern, urban lifestyle for too long.

Women like Alison O'Neill, who owns her own flock of sheep and designs tweed clothing, demonstrate that you can live a life of independence and fulfilment in Britain's remotest regions. There are hardships to be endured but innumerable compensations when the Dales are on your doorstep.

Each chapter features women who made the choice to live and work collaboratively with the people and places of the Yorkshire landscape, whether they be farmers, artists, vets, publicans, entrepreneurs, artisans, academics, curators or vicars. And all have a passion for life.

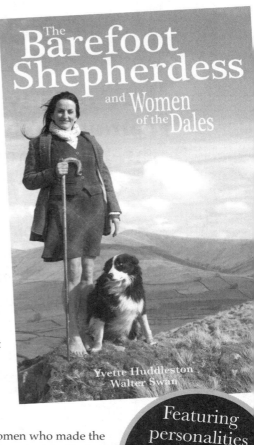

Featuring personalities from the ITV series **The Dales**

Kath Padgett arrived as a naïve, newly-qualified graduate teacher of modern languages just as the pop band Dawn were topping the charts with 'Knock Three Times,' Spangles were the sweets of choice and orange mini skirts with shoes from Freeman, Hardy & Willis all the rage.

'In those first two years, I laughed and cried, encountered wonderful and inspirational people, many of whom turned out to be lifelong friends and, in addition to learning how to teach, was taught how to learn. I learned about strength of character, tough love and the things that really mattered in life.'

This is the story of those early teaching years. The characters and black humour, the rawness, deprivations and an instilling of hope as much as education.

As much a social history of the time – including original letters received from parents – she deals with playground tragedy, first foreign trips and staff room politics, emerging on a career path

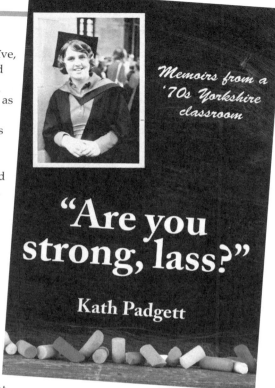

Memoirs from a '70s Yorkshire classroom

"Are you strong, lass?"

Kath Padgett

"My story is in no way all sweetness and light, cute and slushy. It's earthy, gritty and heartbreaking, yet also rewarding, challenging, life-changing and vital..."

that saw her ultimately spend forty-six years as a teacher.

These recollections of inner-city secondary school life in early 1970s Yorkshire are as poignant and entertaining as they are nostalgic.

"Are you strong, lass? Because you'll need to be, working here..."

It was Booker Prize-winning author of *Schindler's Ark*, Thomas Keneally, who described Dave Hadfield as 'The Poet of Rugby League'. True enough, though the man who has also been called Bolton's answer to Bill Bryson has equally revelled in other subjects, like music and travel.

Lost in Spain is the result of the dying wish of Dave's oldest friend's wife, Barb, to have her ashes scattered along the route traced by Laurie Lee when he walked from Gloucestershire to the Med in the 1930s.

That original journey provided the material for *As I Walked Out One Midsummer Morning*, the book upon which, as well as *Cider with Rosie*, Lee's glittering reputation rests.

Lost in Spain is a story of friendship and late-flowering love that is by turns informative, poignant, elegiac and laugh-out-loud funny.

These days freed from the constraints of daily journalism, Hadfield has no plans to stop writing.

Of his ten books so far, five have been written since he was diagnosed with Parkinson's Disease in 2008.

DAVE HADFIELD
IN THE FOOTSTEPS OF LAURIE LEE

Part political intrigue, part comedic travelogue, an incident-packed memoir that bridges the gap between John le Carré and Johnny English....

"Achieves the rare combination of being instructive and funny..." - Rt. Hon. Alan Johnson MP

Paul Knott

The Accidental Diplomat

Adventures in the Foreign Office

Paul Knott is a Northern lad whose working life began on Hull docks, before an improbable career switch to Her Majesty's Diplomatic Service. Here, while globetrotting on official duties, he gets us behind the door of the UK's great offices of state, the Foreign and Commonwealth Office.

Knott's first post is to post-revolutionary Romania, and the eccentricity of a country striving to emerge from the Ceauşescu dictatorship is uproarious.

A superficially more attractive but soulless sojourn in Dubai is enlivened by being abducted at gunpoint by terrorists. His time in the police-state of Uzbekistan is happier, where he takes a hands-on approach to human rights.

A year in Kiev offers a close-up view of the ongoing crisis in Ukraine, plus a few James Bond moments. Finally, he winds up Russia, at a time when an ex-spy is murdered in London by radiation poisoning.

"An unexpectedly engrossing read"
James Brown, Sabotage Times

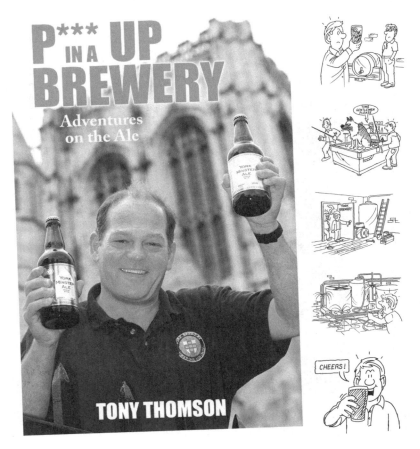

A s well as creating a superior beer, the pioneering indie brewer wanted to offer Minster city visitors an alternative attraction – a showpiece brewery with a visitor centre, bar and club.

P**s Up in a Brewery records every step along the way to building a successful business – from the birth of an idea to the search for funding; from hauling a second-hand kit across the Pennines to the improbable task of finding premises within the city walls; from tackling the stern resistance of York landlords to the industry's most coveted awards.

Alongside the drama is humour. A cast of colourful characters include Tony's partner in crime, one-time burger-flipper Smithy, and the softly-spoken barman who lets his wooden club do the talking. In short, this is something between a soap opera, business plan and sitcom.

Funny Bones
My Life in Comedy
By Freddie 'Parrotface' Davies

with a foreword by Ken Dodd

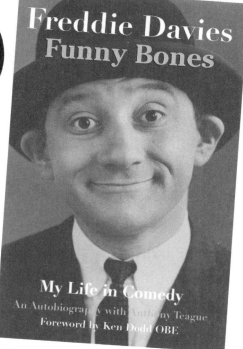

Freddie Davies
Funny Bones

My Life in Comedy
An Autobiography with Anthony Teague
Foreword by Ken Dodd OBE

In 1964, an appearance on TV talent show *Opportunity Knocks* made 'Parrotface' comedian Freddie Davies famous overnight. Spectacular success followed, stars such as Judy Garland, Cliff Richard and Cary Grant, were fans...

When it all began to slip in the 1980s, Freddie became a producer and then forged yet another career as a serious actor. He appeared to great acclaim in a Royal Shakespeare Company production of *The Secret Garden* and cult film *Funny Bones* – alongside Lee Evans and Jerry Lewis – based on tales of Freddie's music hall comic grandfather Jack Herbert.

Fifty years on from his TV debut, Freddie tells his story, revealing the tragedy behind his early days in Salford and family secret that rocked his world. He paints a vivid picture of a gruelling apprenticeship in the Northern clubs – revealing how 'Parrotface' spluttered into life.

With a foreword by the late Ken Dodd, this unique autobiography is a poignant and hilarious evocation of a vanished world, with insights into the art of stand-up. A rich nostalgic treat for comedy connoisseurs.

Available in hardback or paperback

Early on the morning of his 63rd birthday, DAVE HADFIELD walked out of his front door and caught a bus...

Route 63: Around England on a Free Bus Pass

Dave Hadfield

Foreword by Sky Sports presenter Dave Clark

It was the first stage of an epic journey that would take him around the furthest flung corners of his native England, showing it to him from a completely new angle.

Already acclaimed for books on sport and music, Dave Hadfield broadens his canvas in his finest work yet. Heading south along the Welsh Borders, west to Land's End, along the South Coast to Dover, through London and up the eastern side of the country to Newcastle, through the Pennines and the Lakes and back home to Lancashire; he chronicles what he sees and hears on an itinerary that involves over 100 local buses. And he does it all for nothing – on a pass for which he is qualified by Parkinson's Disease.

Undeterred by that disability, he explores the country he loves with a keen eye and fine ear for the absurd. Thoughtful and hilarious, *Route 63* will appeal to all who love the very best in travel writing.

Foreword by Sky Sports presenter Dave Clark

The Woman without a Number

The Woman Without a Number is the inspirational story of holocaust survivor Iby Knill, whose early childhood was spent in Czechoslovakia before her parents – alarmed at the persecution of Jews in Germany – smuggled her over to Hungary.

There, she was caught by the Security Police, imprisoned and tortured, not just for having Jewish connections, but for being in Hungary illegally and aiding the resistance movement. She was sent to the infamous Auschwitz-Birkenau camp.

In June 1944, Iby left Auschwitz-Birkenau by volunteering for labour at a hospital unit where she risked her life protecting the weak and helpless from the gas chambers before being freed by Allied Forces at Easter, 1945.

As seen on BBC Television

The woman without a number

IBY KNILL

An inspirational story of Holocaust survival

A sequel to The Woman Without a Number

The Woman with Nine Lives

IBY KNILL
The Woman with Nine Lives

Just what *is* Yorkshireness...?

Yorkshire ... God's Own County ... The Broad Acres ... the Texas of England ... home to some of the UK's most captivating landscapes, coastlines, food, literature, history, music, tea, film, sport and beer, when Britain's largest county and its residents get you in their grip, you are unlikely to escape soon.

Slouching Towards Blubberhouses is a timely and comical look at a region that is friendly, uncompromising, boastful, blunt and maddeningly self-aware, from the viewpoint both of its chosen ones, who wouldn't live anywhere else, and those who look on in envy – or irritation.

It delves beneath the eeh bah gum clichés of whippets, clogs, flat caps and moth-eaten wallets to explore what really makes Tykes tick.

And it wonders if coming from Yorkshire still means owt in a changing and diverse 21st century.

Slouching Towards Blubberhouses

A (right grand) Tour de Yorkshireness

by Tony Hannan

Adventures in Unpopular Music
By Dave Hadfield

For almost 50 years, Dave Hadfield has followed the genres of music that grabbed his youthful heart and mind. In ALL THE WRONG NOTES, he has written not just a musical memoir, but a personal and social history of the last half-century. Like a Zelig with a finger in his ear, he has been where folk music has happened and describes it, affectionately but warts-and-all, in a way it has never been described before.

Hadfield's sure ear for quirks and eccentricities produces unique takes on major figures like Bob Dylan, Ewan MacColl and Leonard Cohen. It celebrates the foot-soldiers and their role in keeping left-field music alive. Humorous and provocative in equal measure, ALL THE WRONG NOTES is the key to a fascinating world of music.

Investigate our other titles and
stay up to date with all our latest releases at
www.scratchingshedpublishing.co.uk